THE
RULES BOOK
2009-2012

THE
RULES BOOK
2009-2012

ERIC TWINAME
REVISED BY BRYAN WILLIS

ADLARD COLES NAUTICAL
LONDON

Dedication

To my mother and father who taught me the first rule I knew

Published by Adlard Coles Nautical
an imprint of A & C Black (Publishers) Ltd
36 Soho Square, London W1D 3QY
www.adlardcoles.com

Copyright © Eric Twiname 1977, 1981
Copyright © Eric Twiname and Bryan Willis
1985, 1989, 1993, 1997, 2001, 2004, 2009
Rules section © International Sailing Federation 2008

First edition published by Adlard Coles 1977
Reprinted with amendments 1977 (twice)
Reprinted 1978, 1979
Second edition 1981
Reprinted 1984
Third edition 1985
Reprinted 1985
Fourth edition 1989
Reprinted 1989, 1990
Fifth edition published by Adlard Coles Nautical 1993
Sixth edition 1997
Seventh edition 2001
Eighth edition 2005
Ninth edition 2009

ISBN 978-1-4081-0950-2

A CIP catalogue for this book is available from the British Library

A & C Black uses paper produced with elemental chlorine-free pulp,
harvested from managed sustainable forests

Typeset by Falcon Oast Graphic Art Ltd in 8 on 10pt Din Regular
Printed in Spain by GraphyCems

Note: While all reasonable care has been taken in the production of this
publication, the publisher takes no responsibility for the use of the methods
or products described in the book.

CONTENTS

PREFACE

Eric Twiname was an active dinghy sailor, a keen team racer and a Laser National Champion. He liked to look at the rules from the competitor's point of view. He campaigned successfully to get the turns penalty system into the rulebook (before its introduction, boats had to retire whenever they broke a rule) and he'd have been delighted to see that the Two-Turns Penalty is now the standard penalty system in the main body of the rules. He also tried, unsuccessfully, to get the order of the rules changed to put the sections of most interest to the competitor at the front of the book. Twenty years later the rules were reorganised almost exactly as he proposed.

Eric wrote regular rules articles in the 1970s which were so popular that he used the same comic-strip style for his famous *Rules Book*, which he wrote after serving for several years on the Royal Yachting Association's Racing Rules Committee.

It was Eric who persuaded me to join the RYA Racing Rules Committee under the chairmanship of Gerald Sambrooke-Sturgess who, with Greg Bemis from the United States, first developed a set of international racing rules. Eric would be very pleased to see the dramatically simplified rules that came into effect in 1997.

Eric's tragic death in 1980 meant a great loss both to his friends and to racing sailors everywhere. His *Rules Book* has helped countless helmsmen to grasp the principles of the racing rules, and in making the changes necessary for the book to comply with the current rules, I have been careful not to change Eric's unique method of presentation, which is so popular all over the world.

I am grateful to Marianne Middelthon from Norway for checking my updated manuscript.

Bryan Willis

Eric's name and memory live on not only in this book. The Eric Twiname Memorial Trust, a registered charity, helps youngsters start and progress in the sport of sailing. Its address is:

Dinny Reed, Administrator
Eric Twiname Memorial Trust
Sycamore Cottage
Shortheath Common, Kingsley
Borden, Hants GU35 9JS

THE RULE CHANGES

The major differences between the 2005–2008 and the 2009–2012 racing rules.

Every year at the Conference of the International Sailing Federation, improvements and amendments are made to the racing rules, but only every four years (in the year following the Olympic Games) are the 'new rules' published. This ninth edition of *The Rules Book* has been revised to include the changes that came into force on 1 January 2009. Most of the changes are for clarification, but some change the way the game is played.

If you are new to racing and this is your first book on the rules, you really don't need to read this section because comparing what the rules were to what they are now will be of little interest. Move on to the real-life situations, or put the book with your kit ready to refer to it if there is an incident you are unsure about. This section is for sailors who have been racing for a while.

As usual, there are many small changes aimed at making rules easier to understand or less ambiguous.

But there are also a few changes that affect the way the game of sailing is played. I'll start with the important changes and then go on to the ones of interest only to the 'rules gurus':

● The size of 'zones' at marks has been increased to three hull lengths. There is no longer a 'Two-Length Zone', just a 'zone', which is defined as 'The area around a mark within a distance of three hull lengths of the boat nearer to it. A boat is in the zone when any part of her hull is in the zone.' 'Sailing instructions may change to 'two' or 'four', the number of hull lengths determining the zone around marks, provided that the number is the same for all boats using those marks and for all the marks on the course' (Definitions and rule 86.1(b)).

It will be interesting to see how many organizers take up the opportunity of increasing or decreasing the size of the zone for the races under their jurisdiction.

● There is a new definition called 'Mark-Room'. Under the old rules, when a right-of-way boat was required to 'give room' at a mark, the amount of room was 'the space a boat needs in the existing conditions while manoeuvring promptly in a seamanlike way'. The position at which an outside boat had to start giving room was a little vague. Now, as soon as one of the boats is in the zone (three hull lengths), then the outside boat must give sufficient room to the inside boat to 'sail to the mark' in a seamanlike manner. Then, at that moment, the outside boat must give room for the inside boat to sail her proper course around the mark.

Normally the obligation starts when either boat has reached the zone. But there is an important exception. If boats are overlapped, and the outside boat will need to change course before the zone in order to give room, then she must do so; she can't wait till the zone and then claim the three lengths was not enough distance to change course to give room. This is important for asymmetrics or catamarans on opposite tacks at a starboard-hand leeward mark, but may apply to keel boats or even dinghies in light winds when there is a strong tidal stream taking them towards the mark.

● Another important change is that the mark-rounding rules do not apply between a boat that is leaving a mark and one that is approaching it – the normal right-of-way rules apply between them.

● It continues to be the case that at a port-hand windward mark a boat tacking onto starboard tack in the zone must not 'cause the other boat to sail above close-hauled to avoid her or prevent the other boat from passing the mark' and 'shall give Mark-Room if the other boat becomes overlapped inside her', but with the increased size of the zone, it makes a layline approach, when you have to tack, even more difficult.

● Under the old rules having an overlap at two lengths from a non-continuing obstruction (such as a big mooring buoy, or a right-of-way boat, or a shoreline) was as important as it was at a mark. But no one took much notice. The new rules remove the requirement for a boat needing room at an obstruction to be over-lapped at a particular distance from it. Now the only criteria for a keep-clear boat astern trying to get an inside overlap is whether the outside boat is able to give room from the time the overlap began. If she can't, then the inside boat has no right to room (rule 19.2(b)).

   This will be particularly important during the last seconds before a start: when a boat astern tries to get between two other boats, the leeward boat is an obstruction, so the test will be 'Can the windward boat give room from the time the overlap was established?'

● It is now clear that when a right-of-way boat establishes an inside overlap at a continuing obstruction, she has the right to room. Typically the two boats are running along an obstruction, with the boat astern on starboard tack and the boat ahead on port tack. The port-tack boat must keep clear and give room.

● Two boats approaching a mark to be left to starboard.

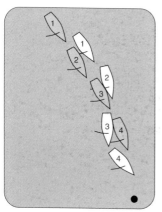

Under the old rules, White broke a rule (at position 2) by sailing below her proper course when Blue was steering a course to leeward of her. That rule has been deleted in the new rules. It is still true of course that when there is an overlap the windward boat must keep clear.

Now to the changes of less interest to most sailors:

- If a boat that is sailing under the racing rules (sailing in or near the racing area and intending to race, is racing, or has been racing) meets a boat that is not (eg a passing cruising boat) the Collision Regulations apply. No change there. But when the racing boat breaks a rule (that is, a rule of the Col Regs), under the old rules another racing boat could not protest (only the race committee or protest committee could), but under the new rules another racing boat can protest (rules Part 2 'When Boats Meet' preamble).

- 'Acceptance of the Rules'. This is a rule that aims to ensure that disputes are resolved within the ISAF system (protest committees, juries, and national authorities' appeal bodies) and ISAF review board, and prohibit taking a dispute to a court of law. The old rule was somewhat confusing (rule 3).

- The anti-doping rule has been simplified; sailors must comply with the rules of the World Anti-Doping Code, the rules of the World Anti-Doping Agency and ISAF Regulation 21, Anti-Doping Code. It continues to be the case that alleged doping violations cannot be protested by a competitor, so sailors other than those who race at a high level need not worry too much about taking prescription or non-prescription drugs that might contain substances on the 'banned list'. However, sailors who compete at a high level need to be very careful if they need to take any drug; they should take advice from a medical specialist (rule 5).

- Sailing the course. A new clause has been added so that organizers need not include a sailing instruction if they use a gate in the course: 'When a boat must pass through a gate she shall pass between the gate marks in the direction of the course from the previous mark' (rule 28).

- The 'Round an End Rule' has been renamed the 'I Flag Rule' and the '20% Penalty Rule' has been renamed the 'Z Flag Rule' (rule 30).

- In the case of the 'Z Flag Rule', it is now clear that if a boat is identified as being in the triangle in the final minute of one start, and then is similarly identified during a subsequent attempt to start the same race, the boat will receive an additional 20% Scoring Penalty (making the total penalty 40% of boats entered), but she can't get a worse score than that given for a DSQ. You must of course be behind the line at the moment of the starting signal or you'll be scored as a non-starter, so even under the 'Z Flag Rule', you must come back if you are over the line at the start (rule 30.2).

  I was at an event in 2006 where the race was shortened after all the boats had passed through the shortened course finishing line (ie retrospectively), causing a lot of unhappiness. A new clause has been added to rule 32.2 'The shortened course shall be signalled before the first boat crosses the finishing line'.

- Four years ago there was a rule requiring trapeze harnesses to have a quick-release mechanism in case of capsize (rule 40.2). This has now been removed because of legal liability problems. That doesn't mean you shouldn't think carefully about what equipment you should use and how it can be released in an emergency, but there is no longer a rule about it.

● 'Personal buoyancy' becomes 'a personal flotation device'. 'When flag Y is displayed with one sound before or with the warning signal, competitors shall wear personal flotation devices . . .' (no change so far, but a phrase has been added), '. . . except briefly while changing or adjusting clothing or personal equipment' (rules 1.2, 27.1, 40 and Signals).

● It is now clear that under a black flag start, there will be no X flag for boats in the triangle (formed by starting line and first mark) in the final minute. They will simply be recorded as DSQ (disqualified) (rules 29.1 and 30.3).

● There is an additional clause in rule 42 (illegal propulsion) to allow sailing instructions to permit the use of engines in certain circumstances (eg to get through shipping lanes or avoid a tanker) 'provided the boat does not gain a significant advantage in the race'. Sailing instructions for some events have been making such a provision for years, but until now rule 42 was not a rule that could be changed by the sailing instructions (new rule 42.3(h)).

● The rules for taking a penalty at the time of the incident (two turns for breaking a 'When Boats Meet' rule and one turn for touching a mark) have been reorganized to be much clearer, but nothing has changed (rule 44).

● At some events the sailing instructions provides for a scoring penalty in place of the Two-Turns Penalty. The rules for taking a scoring penalty have been rewritten to make it clear that the boat takes the penalty by displaying the yellow flag. She cannot subsequently change her mind (rule 44.3).

● Two clarifications about ballast for readers who sail keel-boats. It is now clear (if it wasn't before) that sails not hoisted are included in the restrictions on moving ballast (you mustn't move ballast for the purpose of changing trim or stability). And it is now clear (if it wasn't before) that it is permitted to bail out bilge water that has accidentally come aboard (rule 51).

● It is now clear that the race committee or the protest committee may act on a report from the representative of a boat admitting a rule breach (eg starting engines during a race). Previously the race committee and protest committee were not allowed to act on a report from an 'interested party' so strictly speaking they could not act on such a report (rule 60.2(a) and 60.3(a)).

● A boat can no longer seek redress claiming an improper action or omission of the protest committee when the boat was a party to the hearing that made the decision which is the subject of the redress claim. She had the opportunity to make her arguments in the original hearing, so she shouldn't have a second chance (rule 62.1(a)). She can still request a reopening, though, if she believes the protest committee has made a significant error or there is significant new evidence. However, it is for the protest committee to decide whether the circumstances warrant such a reopening (rule 66).

● There is now a rule that requires any member of a protest committee who realizes he is an 'interested party' not to take any further part in the hearing, although he may appear as a witness. A new phrase requires such people to declare any possible self-interest as soon as they are aware of it (rule 63.4). Personally I see no problem in a committee member who declares an interest, if both parties are adults and agree to his continued membership.

● There is some new wording to make it clear that when the protest committee decides that a boat has broken a rule, but the boat has taken an applicable penalty, she shall not be penalized further with respect to the same incident (unless the penalty for the rule broken is a disqualification that shall not be excluded from the boat's score) (rule 64.1(b)).

● There are also several re-wordings providing protest committees with details about what to do if a party does not show up at a rule 69 hearing, and how to report any findings (rule 69).

    In the past, if there was an appeal against a protest committee's decision or procedure, it had to go to the 'National Authority of the Event' – this is pretty obvious if it is your local club, but not so obvious if it is a passage race between countries. So the new rules include the phrase 'if boats will pass through the waters of more than one national authority while racing, the sailing instructions shall identify the national authority to which appeals or requests may be sent' (rule 70.3).

● Some event organizers and Class Associations want their events to be restricted to amateur sailors. As a result, the ISAF Sailor Classification Code was created as a service to provide events and classes with an international system for classification of sailors. The Code classifies sailors into three groups based on financial involvement in boat racing and/or the use in the sailor's work of knowledge or skill capable of improving the performance of a boat in a race. It is not based on racing success, prowess or talent. A new rule has been added for those events that use the system: 'If the notice of race or class rules state that some or all competitors must satisfy classification requirements, the classification shall be carried out as described in ISAF Regulation 22, Sailor Classification Code.' Sailors can obtain a classification by visiting www.sailing.org/classification (rule 79).

● There is a new rule that may affect many sailing clubs and other event organizers: 'The sailing instructions may change a class rule only when the class rules permit the change, or when written permission of the class association for the change is displayed on the official notice board' (rule 87).

- The new rules define an 'international event' as 'an event where entries from other countries are expected'. At such an event, sailors can expect to be provided with sailing instructions in English.

- There are some changes to the penalty system (described in Appendix P) used by judges on the water looking for breaches of rule 42 (propulsion). (A judge penalizes a boat by waving a yellow flag, blowing a whistle, and pointing to the boat and hailing the boat's sail number.) For the first occasion the boat must take a Two-Turns Penalty, and for the second occasion she must retire. No change there. But for the third penalty she must retire from the race and be disqualified and must count that disqualification in her overall score (DNE). The change is that she used not to be allowed to sail again, but now she can, albeit carrying a 'retired' score, and a non-excludable DSQ. At least she can sail rather than getting up to mischief on shore during the subsequent races. Personally I believe any sailor given a penalty three times in one regatta for breaking rule 42, should be investigated for a 'gross breach' under rule 69 (Gross misconduct). That person surely knew he or she was breaking the rule on the third occasion, if not the second or the first. By the way, while we're on the subject, if you sail in events where there is 'on the water judging of rule 42' I strongly recommend that every time you are penalized for breaking the rule, you ask the judge (between races or onshore after racing) for an explanation. Take your coach with you if you have one. If you do not know which judge it was, ask the jury chairman to organize a meeting. You cannot get the decision overturned (other than the exception below), but you can find out how the judges think – which when it comes to rule 42 is more important than what you or your coach think. Or you might even convince the judges that they've got it wrong and change how they think for the future.

- The highly commendable system of switching parts of rule 42 off and on depending on the wind-strength, which some classes have adopted, is now included in the Appendix:

    (a) If the class rules permit pumping, rocking and ooching when the wind speed exceeds a specified limit, the race committee may signal that those actions are permitted, as specified in the class rules, by displaying flag 'O' before or with the warning signal. The flag shall be removed at the starting signal.

    (b) If the wind speed exceeds the specified limit after the starting signal, the race committee may display flag 'O' with repetitive sounds at a rounding mark to signal that the actions are permitted, as specified in the class rules, to a boat after she has passed the mark.

    (c) If the wind speed becomes less than the specified limit after flag 'O' was displayed, the race committee may display flag 'R' with repetitive sounds at a rounding mark to signal that rule 42, as changed by the class rules, applies to a boat after she has passed the mark (Appendix P5).

It is reasonable to treat the rule 42 on-the-water judges as umpires and make their decisions not open to protest, but there have been occasions in the 470 and Finn classes when the flag 'O' was being displayed by the race committee, meaning that pumping, rocking and ooching were permitted (in accordance with class rules), but the judges didn't know flag 'O' was being displayed and penalized a boat. So there is a new clause in Appendix P: 'A boat shall not be given redress for an action by a member of the protest committee or its designated observer under rule P1 unless the action was improper due to a failure to take into account a race committee signal or a class rule' (rule P4).

- The term 'Fetching' is now defined (because it is used in rules 18 and 20 about Marks and Obstructions): 'A boat is fetching a mark when she is in a position to pass to windward of it and leave it on the required side without changing tack' (Definitions).

LEARNING
THE RULES

The rules of sailing are complex. There's no getting away from that. But there are ways of making rule knowledge much more accessible and the rules themselves easier to understand. This book is written very much with those two aims in mind.

A good working knowledge

Anyone who races sailing boats needs to know something about the rules. To begin with you need to know only enough to get your boat around the course without fouling the others. Later, the rules become tactically important because they define what moves you can make when trying to overtake other boats and, just as important, what tricks other people might legitimately use in trying to overtake you.

So the crucial point about learning the sailing rules is that you need a sound working knowledge. There is little point in learning the rules merely to be able to quote chapter and verse. That won't help you on the water, whereas a good working knowledge certainly will, since knowing the rules is a vital part of your racing skills – as important as knowledge of wind and weather.

The International Sailing Federation's (ISAF) racing rulebook is something most people approach at best reluctantly. For one thing it's only usually approached at all when you've got a problem; which puts it immediately into the category of garages, police stations and dentists. But with the difference that often when you turn to the rulebook, you will find something that either you can't quite understand or that contradicts something you thought you knew.

After an incident, you need to make a decision quickly; take a penalty or sail on and risk being disqualified after a protest hearing. Making the right decision could determine whether you win a major regatta or championship.

Which rule applies?

This book approaches this problem by looking at real live situations that you're likely to come across while racing. So rather than looking for a rule which might apply to the situation in question, you can turn straight to that situation and read which rule applies, how it applies and why. To make this possible, the situations are arranged here, not in the order set out in the ISAF rule book, but to a logic based on your perception of situations as you meet them on the water.

There are several things that anyone who knows anything at all about sailing will be able to tell you about a collision or near miss, whether they have ever seen a rule book or not. The first thing they'll be able to say is *whereabouts on the course the incident happened*. They shouldn't find it too difficult, either, to say *which tacks the boats were on* (port tack or starboard tack), *whether they were overlapped, and whether either boat was changing course*. And already, by answering these questions correctly, the majority of racing incidents can be resolved and we are left with, at most, ten per cent. The sections of the book have therefore been arranged to correspond to parts of the course, with subdivisions into incidents where boats are on opposite tacks, on the same tack, changing course or rounding a mark.

In this way, when you are trying to unravel the rights and wrongs of a particular incident, you can quickly focus on the relevant five or ten per cent of possible incidents. Among these, the one you want will be easy to find. Having found it, you can read why one boat is in the right and the other in the wrong, why a particular rule applies, which rule that is and, on difficult points, which appeals cases support the interpretation. The rule referred to can then be looked up in the ISAF Racing Rules of Sailing (reproduced at the back of this book).

Avoiding breaking a rule

So far I have only mentioned the book's use in providing a post-mortem analysis after a rule has been broken. But if you're a racing helmsman you constantly need to know just what you can do during a race without breaking any rules. You can certainly build up this knowledge by tearing around the course hitting other boats and being protested against afterwards, but by far the best way to learn is to keep your rule knowledge running in advance of your sailing skills.

Some right-of-way problems are much more common than others, so the racing situations dealt with here have been graded so that you can, if you like, sit down and work up your rule knowledge to a suitable level that fits in with your other racing abilities.

How to use this book

The incidents and situations interpreted in the book are graded on three levels with symbols for quick recognition. These levels are:

1   Rules everyone who races should know (dealt with on pages 13 to 18)

2   Racing at the top end of a club fleet

3   Top-level national and international competition and team racing

For the purpose of learning the rules, the book should not be read from cover to cover in the usual way. That would be too big a bite at once and probably pretty confusing, unless you already know the rules quite well. Instead, the best approach is to decide what level of rule knowledge you want from the book beforehand, then to ignore everything listed beyond the level you've set yourself.

Take the example of a helmsman who has raced for a couple of seasons, and who wants to improve his rule knowledge so that it is at least on a par with the people who are winning his club races. His approach to learning would be to read all items marked by one boat (but not those marked by two boats), checking back to any rules referred to, but ignoring the appeal case references.

If you work this way you needn't read from the front of the book to the back but will learn faster by picking a particular section – mark-rounding from an off-wind leg, for example – and first studying only that section, rather than trying to take in too much at once. Re-reading, dipping into the book at random – but not yet reading beyond the level you've set yourself – are all useful parts of the learning process. For really keen groups of people, and particularly for young sailors, quizzes are an obvious way of livening up the process.

Learning is also speeded up considerably by using the book as a reference after racing to check the rights and wrongs of any incidents or near misses you experienced during the race. When using the book in this way, of course, you would not restrict yourself to the grading levels, since an incident you want to know about might be one of those rare ones in group 3.

One important word of warning, though. What may look like two identical situations in different sections of the book will sometimes have opposite interpretations. This is because the position on the course is crucial. For example, when two boats collide within three lengths of a mark, the boat in the wrong might be the one that is in the right if you take the mark away and have them in open water on a leg of the course. It is often vital to make sure you bear in mind the leg of the course the boats are on – which is why that information is printed at the top of every page.

The interpretations

The interpretations used are, as far as possible, not my own but those of the ISAF. Throughout, I have included references to ISAF's most useful published appeals, so anyone can look these up if they want to. At a protest meeting – whether you are on the committee or one of the parties in conflict – the relevant appeal case placed on the table is usually decisive. You are instantly a rule expert. No longer is it a question of 'my opinion is this . . .' but 'this is what the definitive ISAF case says', which is difficult for a protest committee to refute, or for a competitor who has just been disqualified to argue about.

The ISAF appeal cases are accepted as definitive throughout the world. Major sailing nations also publish cases resulting from appeals and questions they have decided, to help guide the clubs and race organizers in the area of their jurisdiction. Although national authorities' cases do not have the same 'authoritative' status as the ISAF cases, a protest committee that decides a case contrary to a case published by its own national authority is obviously likely to have the decision overturned on appeal.

Where to obtain the ISAF rules

The rules themselves are revised once every four years and those used in this edition are valid until the end of 2012. These rules together with the RYA prescriptions can be bought in a booklet from the Royal Yachting Association, Romsey Road, Eastleigh, Hampshire SO5 4YA, England. So can the RYA appeals case book. The ISAF racing rules alone and the ISAF Cases can be bought from the International Sailing Federation at Ariadne House, Town Quay, Southampton, SO14 2AQ United Kingdom. The current text of the rules is on the ISAF web site: www.sailing.org.

THE RULES EVERYONE WHO RACES SHOULD KNOW

An understanding of these first few pages of introduction to the rules enables a racing helmsman to keep out of trouble and provides the logical framework which underlies all the 'when boats meet' rules, however complex. These are the most important five pages in the book.

The sailing rules are designed to prevent collisions and to facilitate fair sailing. So when boats collide, or when a right-of-way boat is forced to steer clear to avoid contact, the boat in the wrong should be penalized. The voluntary penalty is the 'Two-Turns Penalty' (two turns of the boat). If a helmsman in the wrong does not take the voluntary penalty soon after the incident, another competitor may lodge a protest. In the protest meeting the boat in the wrong is disqualified. The basic right-of-way code is quite simple, but it is important to know that the rights and obligations of boats in open water are often different from those at marks of the course or obstructions.

Basic right-of-way

I A boat on port tack must keep clear of a boat on starboard tack (rule 10).

2 A windward boat must keep clear of a leeward boat (rule 11).

3 A boat that is tacking must keep clear of one that is not (rule 13).

4 A boat clear astern of another must keep clear of the one ahead when they are both on the same tack (rule 12).

Basics at a windward mark

At a windward mark – that is a mark of the course that you have been tacking to get to – the basics are:

1 When on opposite tacks, take the mark away and apply only the basic right-of-way rules (rules 10 and 18.1(a) and (b)).

2 When on the same tack, the boat next to the mark must be given room to sail to it and round or pass the mark by the boat outside (rule 18.2 (a)).

3 When a boat is tacking to pass the mark, she must keep clear of any other boat (rules 13 and 18.3).

4 A leeward boat overlapping on the outside must give a boat on the inside room to tack (rule 18.2(a) and Definition of Mark-Room).

Basics at a downwind mark

starboard boat
must give room

inside boat is
entitled to room

At a downwind mark – one you have sailed to on a reach or a run – the basics are:

1 If the boat on the inside at the mark is the keep-clear boat (on port tack if they are on opposite tacks, or to windward if they are on the same tack), she must be given Mark-Room (rule 18.2(a)).

2 If the boat on the inside at the mark is the right-of-way boat (on starboard tack if they are on opposite tacks, or to leeward if they are on the same tack), the outside boat must also keep clear (rules 10 and 11). But the inside boat must not sail further from the mark than needed to sail her proper course if her course around the mark is to gybe (rule 18.4).

3 If a boat is clear ahead when she reaches the zone (see page 52), the other boat must give her room to sail to the mark and then her proper course round it, as long as she does not leave the zone nor pass head to wind (rules 18.2(b) and 18.2(c)).

4 If the boats are overlapped when one of them reaches the zone, the outside boat must give the inside boat room to sail to the mark and then sail her proper course round it (as long as the inside boat does not leave the zone nor pass head to wind). She must do so even if the overlap is broken inside the zone (rules 18.2(b) and 18.2(c)).

The rule stops applying if either boat passes head to wind.

Basic rights before and at the start

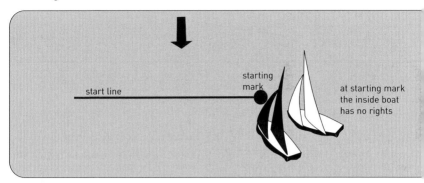

When milling about before a start, it is important to realize that if you are out of control or are preoccupied in adjusting a halyard, you can be penalized in a collision with a boat that has right-of-way. So if you're going to mess about with your boat before the start, make sure you're on starboard tack and keep a good lookout for boats approaching to leeward. If you break a rule in the 'preparatory period' (usually the four minutes before the start), you will have to take a Two-Turns Penalty as soon as possible after the incident. (If you break a rule before the preparatory signal, there is no penalty unless you cause damage, in which case you may have to pay for it.)

The rules about giving room at marks change when boats are 'approaching the line to start'. No boat has the right to room at a starting mark when approaching the line to start (unless the mark is not surrounded by navigable water).

Changing course

Whenever a right-of-way boat changes course, she must usually give the keep-clear boat 'room to keep clear'. Sometimes a boat is not allowed to sail above her proper course, but when a boat establishes an overlap on your windward side you may luff right up to head-to-wind provided that you give the windward boat room to keep clear (rule 16).

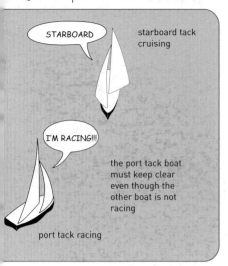

STARBOARD

starboard tack cruising

I'M RACING!!!

the port tack boat must keep clear even though the other boat is not racing

port tack racing

Boats cruising, boats in other races and motor boats

The racing rules apply only between boats that are racing, either in the same or different races. When a boat that is racing meets one that is cruising, a different set of rules apply: they are the International Regulations for Preventing Collisions at Sea (IRPCAS). Although essentially the same as the basic racing rules, there are some important differences. The IRPCAS do not allow luffing an overtaking boat, and a boat that is overtaking must keep clear, regardless of which tacks the boats are on. IRPCAS give no rights to boats that are rounding or passing marks or obstructions. As a matter of courtesy, boats not racing should do their best to keep clear of those racing, but there are no rules requiring them to do so.

Sailing boats have right-of-way over motor boats, but in confined waters, ships have right-of-way over sailing boats. It should always be remembered that the racing rules are primarily intended to enable boats to manoeuvre closely without colliding.

DEFINITIONS AND TERMS

The rules are built on simple and precise ideas; these are the building blocks and they must be understood if the full meaning of the rules is to become clear.

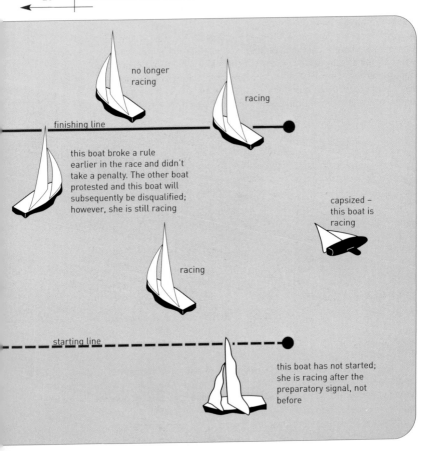

no longer racing

racing

finishing line

this boat broke a rule earlier in the race and didn't take a penalty. The other boat protested and this boat will subsequently be disqualified; however, she is still racing

capsized – this boat is racing

racing

starting line

this boat has not started; she is racing after the preparatory signal, not before

Racing

The racing rules apply to boats that are racing or sailing in or near the racing area and intend to race or have been racing. Penalties for breaking the 'when boats meet' rules come into force at the preparatory signal (usually 4 minutes before the starting signal) and apply to a boat until she has finished and cleared the finishing line and marks. A boat not racing (before the preparatory signal or after finishing and clearing the line and marks) is subject to the racing rules but will be penalized only if she interferes with a boat that is racing (Part 2 preamble and rule 23.1).

A boat that breaks a rule without realizing it and that therefore continues racing and is later disqualified after a protest has exactly the same rights under the rules as other boats racing (ISAF Case 1). A boat that continues to race without taking a penalty, knowing that she has broken a rule, violates the basic principle: Sportsmanship and the Rules.

Port tack and starboard tack

A boat is on starboard tack when her starboard side is her windward side. Conversely, a boat is on port tack when her port side is her windward side. However, when sailing directly downwind or by the lee, she is on the tack corresponding to the opposite of her mainsail. Sailors who have problems knowing which tack they are on can usefully paint 'starboard tack' on the starboard side of the boom and 'port tack' on the port side. It saves having to think (Definitions).

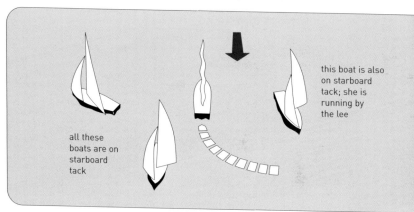

this boat is also on starboard tack; she is running by the lee

all these boats are on starboard tack

Close-hauled

The term 'close-hauled' defines a direction of sailing in relation to the wind; the angle from the wind is different for different classes of boat and, to a lesser degree, among boats of the same class with different wind speeds, boat speeds, and sailing style.

close-hauled port tack

close-hauled starboard tack

Windward and leeward

'A boat's leeward side is the side that is or, when she is head to wind, was away from the wind. However, when sailing by the lee or directly downwind, her leeward side is the side on which her mainsail lies. The other side is her windward side.
When two boats on the same tack overlap, the one on the leeward side of the other is the leeward boat. The other is the windward boat' (Definitions).

Luffing

A boat is luffing when she is changing course towards the wind. Other phrases commonly used to mean the same as luffing are: 'hardening up', 'pointing up' and 'putting the helm down'.

Bearing away

A boat that is bearing away is changing course away from the wind. Other phrases commonly used are: 'bearing off', 'bearing down', 'freeing off' and 'putting the helm up'.

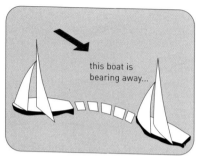

this boat is bearing away...

...so is this one

Clear astern and clear ahead; overlap

'One boat is clear astern of another when her hull and equipment in normal position are behind a line abeam from the aftermost point of the other boat's hull and equipment in normal position. The other boat is clear ahead.'

Romeo

Juliet is clear ahead

Juliet

Romeo

Juliet

Romeo now has an overlap

Romeo is forward of this line so the boats are over-lapped

Romeo

Juliet

'Boats overlap when neither is clear astern or when a boat between them overlaps both' (Definitions).

Juliet is not overlapped on the imaginary line at right angles to Romeo's rudder but...

Juliet

Romeo

...Romeo and Juliet overlap because each is overlapped on the boat between them

Juliet

Romeo

Juliet is not overlapped on Romeo here because this time the third boat is not between them

Luffing rights

'Luffing rights' is a colloquial term. A boat is said to have 'luffing rights' over a boat to windward when she has the right to sail above her proper course even if it forces the boat to windward to change course to keep clear. Any leeward boat has luffing rights unless she became overlapped from clear astern within two of her hull lengths. Remember that there is no proper course before the starting signal, so before the starting signal any leeward boat has luffing rights. But if she became overlapped from clear astern then at the moment of the start, if she is sailing above her proper course, she must bear away. If the leeward boat changes course she must give room to the windward boat to keep clear, and if the windward boat has the right to Mark-Room at a mark or room at an obstruction, the leeward boat must give room.

Obstruction

An obstruction is 'an object that a boat could not pass without changing course substantially, if she were sailing directly towards it and one of her hull lengths from it. An object that can be safely passed on only one side and an area so designated by the sailing instructions are also obstructions. However, a boat racing is not an obstruc-

to these boats, Bulldozer is an obstruction

Bulldozer – right-of-way boat

tion to other boats unless they are required to keep clear of her or give her room or Mark-Room or, if rule 22 (avoiding a capsized boat) applies, avoid her. A vessel under way, including a boat racing, is never a continuing obstruction' (Definitions). Obstructions include shorelines, heavy patches of weed, fishing nets, shallows (real or perceived), moored boats, tankers, cruising boats and, in some situations, other boats racing.

Mark

A mark is 'an object the sailing instructions require a boat to leave on a specified side, and a race committee boat surrounded by navigable water from which the starting or finishing line extends. An anchor line and objects attached temporarily or accidentally to a mark is not part of it' (Definitions).

A mark's ground tackle is not counted as part of the mark, but when a boat runs into the mooring line and is drawn on to any part of the mark itself, above or below water, she is counted as having hit the mark.

Starting and finishing

'A boat starts when after her starting signal any part of her hull, crew or equipment first crosses the starting line...' She finishes 'when any part of her hull, or crew or equipment in normal position, crosses the finishing line in the direction of the course from the last mark, either for the first time or after taking a penalty... after correcting an error made at the finishing line.'

Starting is dealt with at the beginning of the section on starting (page 27) and finishing is dealt with at the beginning of the section on finishing (page 81).

Postponement and abandonment

A postponed race is delayed before its scheduled start but may be started or abandoned later.

The race committee may abandon a race after it has started only for certain specific reasons. It may reschedule an abandoned race or cancel it. After one boat has sailed the course and finished within the time limit, if any, the race committee shall not abandon the race without considering the consequences for all boats in the race or series (rule 32).

Contact

A collision happens when there is contact between any part of one boat (including all rigging, sails and sheets) or her crew and any part of another boat or her crew.

Proper course

Although a boat is never required to sail her proper course, in some situations a boat is required to not sail 'higher than her proper course'. A proper course is any course a boat would sail to finish as soon as possible in the absence of the other boats referred to in the rule using the term (Definitions).

The reference to 'the other boats referred to in the rule' means that a boat required 'not to sail above her proper course' may, for example, change course to clear her wind or to gain a tactical advantage over another boat or boats ahead or behind.

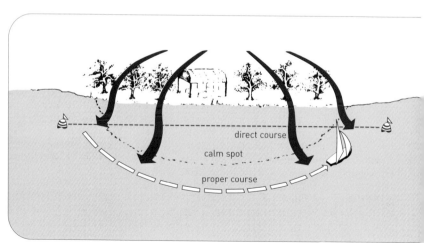

direct course

calm spot

proper course

direction of next mark

proper course for this boat as she luffs prior to surfing down a wave may well be 15 or 20 degrees higher than the average straight line course to the next mark

Proper course refers to the course the boat makes good and not the direction she is pointing, and provided that it is a reasonable choice, a boat's proper course is whatever her helmsman considers is the best course (ISAF Case 14).

There is no proper course before the starting signal.

strong tide

light wind

Crabber is sailing her proper course and has to point well above the mark to do so

heading

proper course

course made good

direction to next mark

Crabber

Boat

The racing rules use the word 'boat' to mean any racing sailing boat (sailboards, Optimists, Lasers and 505s, Ocean Racers, Multihulls, remote-controlled models).

strong tide and light wind

heading

course made good

proper course

direction to next mark

Crabber has to head above the mark to sail her proper course

THE
START

The period covered in this section runs from the preparatory signal until after starting and clearing the starting line.

Starting

A boat *starts* when, having been entirely on the pre-start side of the starting line at or after her starting signal, and having complied with rule 30.1 if it applies, any part of her hull, crew or equipment crosses the starting line in the direction of the first *mark* (Definition of Start).

Timing of starts

The start of a race is signalled by a 5-minute warning signal, a 4-minute preparatory signal, a 1-minute signal, and the starting signal. The sailing instructions may specify a different time (eg 10 minutes) for the warning signal.

The timing is taken from the visual signals, not from the sound signals, which might fail (rule 26).

From the time of the preparatory signal, until after finishing and clearing the finishing line and marks, breaking a 'when boats meet' rule can be exonerated by doing a Two-Turns Penalty (Definition of Racing and Part 2 preamble).

Starting lines

A starting line will usually be one of the following:

(a) A line between a mark and a mast on the committee boat or a place clearly identified in the sailing instructions (1).

(b) A line between two marks (2).

(c) The extension of a line through two stationary posts (3), which may have a mark at or near its outer limit, that boats must pass inside (4).

Inner distance mark (IDM)

On starting lines of types (1), (3) and (4) an inner distance mark may be laid, but this will have an effect only if the sailing instructions state what the obligations of boats are (for example 'boats shall pass between the IDM and the outer starting mark' or 'boats shall not pass between the IDM and the committee boat'). Unless the sailing instructions state otherwise, before you are 'approaching the line from its pre-course side to start', you can pass either side of it (rule 28.2).

Over the line at the start

When any part of a boat, her sails, rigging, equipment or crew is on the course side of the start line at the starting signal, she is said to be 'OCS' (on course side). Usually a boat that is OCS is allowed to return and start properly (rule 29.1).

When one or more boats are OCS, the race committee must make a sound signal and display flag X unless the only boats on the wrong side are so far over that they will not be confused by the absence of a recall signal.

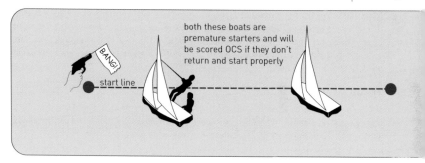

both these boats are premature starters and will be scored OCS if they don't return and start properly

start line

A boat that has crossed the line prematurely must re-start or be scored as 'OCS'. But a premature starter who does not realize her error may be granted redress if she does not return when the visual signal is not accompanied by the prescribed sound signal (rule 29.1 and ISAF Case 31).

When a recalled boat has returned completely to the pre-start side of the starting line, she can start correctly. Flag X is lowered once the last of the premature starters has returned to the pre-start side of the line, or four minutes after the starting signal or one minute before any later starting signal, whichever is the earlier (rule 29.1).

Any boat anchored before the start with part of her ground tackle on the course side of the starting line at the start signal becomes a premature starter because the anchor and warp are part of the boat's equipment (rule 29.1).

When flag I has been displayed as the preparatory signal, any boat whose hull, equipment or crew is on the course side of the starting line during the minute before her starting signal must sail back around either end of the line before starting (she can't just dip back over the line) (rule 30.1).

When flag Z has been displayed as the preparatory signal, any boat whose hull, equipment or crew is in the triangle formed by the starting line and the first mark during the minute before her starting signal will be penalized with a 20% penalty unless the race is postponed or abandoned before the starting signal. If there is no 'general recall' she will be scored as 'OCS' unless she returns and starts properly. If she returns, she will still be penalised by 20% (rule 30.2).

When the black flag has been displayed, any boat whose hull, equipment or crew is in the triangle formed by the starting line and the first mark during the minute before her starting signal will be disqualified without a hearing, and if the race is restarted, she cannot start in the restarted race (rule 30.3).

Hitting a starting mark

A boat that makes contact with a starting mark after the preparatory signal must immediately sail clear of other boats and take a One-Turn Penalty, including a tack and a gybe. If she believes she was forced to hit the mark because of another boat breaking a rule, she need not do the turn. If a boat hits a mark and in the same incident breaks a 'when boats meet' rule, she may exonerate herself by immediately sailing clear and taking only a Two-Turns Penalty.

The Two-Turns Penalty for breaking a rule before the starting signal

When a boat breaks a 'when boats meet' rule after the preparatory signal, she may exonerate herself by taking a Two-Turns Penalty at the first reasonable opportunity after the breach. This means sailing clear of other boats to find a space, and while keeping clear, turning the boat twice in the same direction including two tacks and two gybes. (The Two-Turns Penalty is dealt with in detail on pages 88–9.)

Breaking a rule just before the starting signal will therefore result in a much more severe penalty than a breach soon after the preparatory signal. If a boat breaks a rule just before the starting signal and is also OCS, she must get clear and do her turns as soon as possible, then return behind the line and re-start.

It is two seconds after the starting signal and all these port-tackers have broken rule 10. They must do their turns as soon as they can. Eager Beaver was OCS at the start and will have to go back behind the line and start after completing her turns; Gottawatch started before she broke a rule so she can take her turns and sail on; Simple Simon starts as he commences his turns so he too can complete his turns and sail on.

Anchored, moored, tied up or still ashore

A boat may be disqualified for being ashore, moored or tied up after the preparatory (4-minute) signal (rule 45). If she doesn't sail about in the vicinity of the starting line at some time between the preparatory and starting signals or does not start, she is scored DNC (did not come to the starting area) or DNS (did not start) (Appendix A).

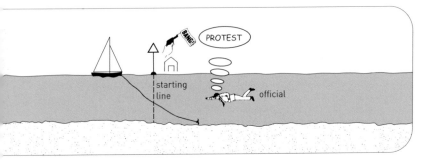

A boat may be anchored after the preparatory signal or held by a member of the crew standing in the water, and no rule is broken (rule 45). However, if an anchor is on the course side of the line at the starting signal, the boat will be scored OCS.

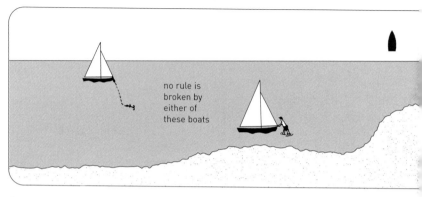

no rule is broken by either of these boats

General recall

When the race officer can't identify boats that are OCS, or when the start is unsatisfactory in some other way, he can make a 'general recall' signal by flying the First Substitute and making two more sounds after the starting signal.

The procedure when the race officer is ready to re-start is:

1 First Substitute is lowered with a sound signal.
2 After one minute, a new warning signal is made (with a flag and sound signal).

First Substitute

Any boat that breaks a rule in the race in which the start is abandoned is not barred from competing in any subsequent starts, and will not be penalized unless the breach happened on the course side of the starting line in the minute before a 'black flag' start (rules 30.3 and 36).

Postponement

A race may be postponed by flying the Answering Pennant with two sounds. The warning signal is made one minute after the Answering Pennant is lowered, accompanied by sound. If there is to be a long delay, the race committee can add a numeral pennant under the AP to indicate the number of hours delay, counted from the scheduled starting time.

Answering Pennant

RIGHT OF WAY

No room at a starting mark

When approaching the line to start, a windward boat (White) is not entitled to room from any leeward boat (Black) at a starting mark that is surrounded by navigable water (Section C preamble). ▶

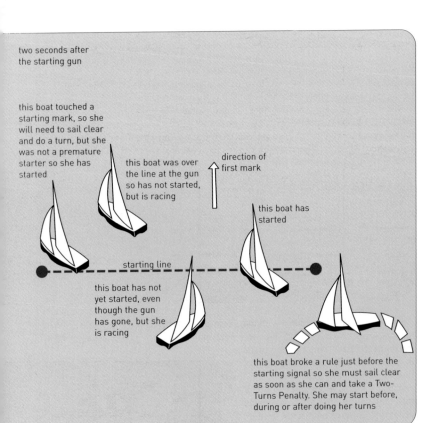

two seconds after the starting gun

this boat touched a starting mark, so she will need to sail clear and do a turn, but she was not a premature starter so she has started

this boat was over the line at the gun so has not started, but is racing

direction of first mark

this boat has started

starting line

this boat has not yet started, even though the gun has gone, but she is racing

this boat broke a rule just before the starting signal so she must sail clear as soon as she can and take a Two-Turns Penalty. She may start before, during or after doing her turns

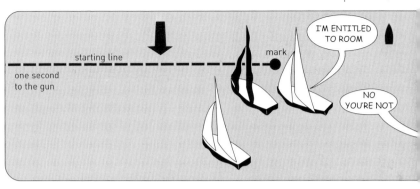

White is not entitled to room but if Black luffs, she must give White room to keep clear (rule 16). With the mark so close, if Black luffs now, White would not be able to keep clear without hitting the mark, so Black must not luff.

If the leeward boat is sailing above close-hauled at the starting signal and she became overlapped from clear astern, she must immediately bear away to close-hauled (assuming that the first leg is a beat) (rule 17 and the Definition of Proper Course).

In the to-ing and fro-ing in the minutes before the start, a windward boat is entitled to room at a starting mark; the 'no room' rule applies only when approaching a starting mark to start (if the starting mark is surrounded by navigable water) (Section C preamble).

At the port end of the starting line, if the mark is surrounded by navigable water, the leeward boat is not entitled to 'room' but as she is the right-of-way boat, she may sail as high as she likes provided that if she luffs she gives the windward boat room to keep clear (rules 11 and 16.1).

The position is quite different if the starting mark is not surrounded by navigable water or the line's length is limited by, say, a pier. A windward boat is then entitled to room at that mark or pier (Part 2, Section C preamble and rule 18.2).

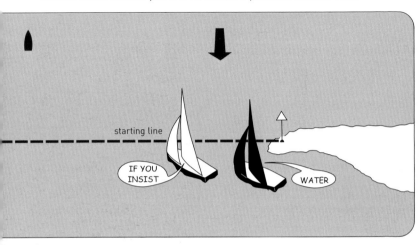

Changing course to start

A right-of-way boat that changes course must give a keep-clear boat room to keep clear. Here Go-getter luffs up to close-hauled to get a good start, but hits a port-tacker that was keeping clear. Go-getter must take a penalty (rule 16.1).

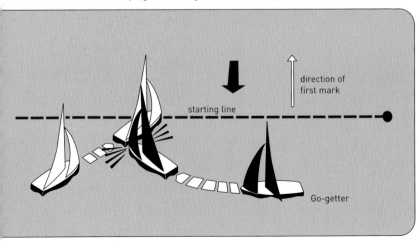

Luffing before the start

Before the starting signal, any leeward boat may luff up to head-to-wind. (If she passes beyond head-to-wind, she'll become a tacking boat). However, any change of course must be such that the windward boat is able to keep clear. If there's something to windward of the windward boat preventing her from responding, the leeward boat might not be able to luff at all (rule 16.1).

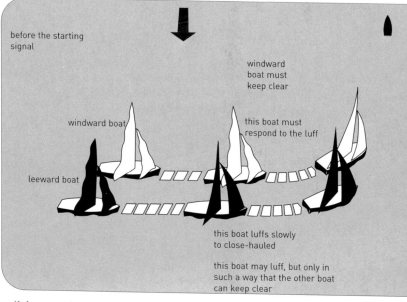

before the starting signal

windward boat must keep clear

windward boat

this boat must respond to the luff

leeward boat

this boat luffs slowly to close-hauled

this boat may luff, but only in such a way that the other boat can keep clear

If, for example, the windward boat was 'dead in the water' (not moving and sails not drawing) when the luff began, she must be given time and space to pull her sail in, gather way and respond to the luff. The leeward boat has to give her this opportunity. It is important to remember that the first movement of the windward boat's stern in responding to a luff is inevitably towards the leeward boat. The windward boat would not be disqualified in a pre-start luffing incident if she was keeping clear and then made every reasonable effort to avoid the leeward boat's luff from the moment the luff began.

When more than one boat is overlapped and the leeward boat luffs, they must all respond, each responding to the luff of the boat immediately to leeward, but each leeward boat must luff in such a way that the boat to windward is able to keep clear.

Over the line at the start

While a boat that has been scored OCS (on the course side at the start) is sailing the course, she carries her normal rights. But at the moment she begins heading back towards the starting line, she must keep clear of boats that are not returning. The normal right-of-way rules apply between two boats both returning (rule 21.1).

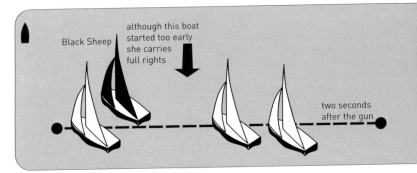

Black Sheep lets her sails flap to slow down, but she maintains her rights until she is heading back towards the line or its extension (rule 21.1).

Once back on the pre-start side of the line, Black Sheep gets back her rights, but she must give any keep-clear boat a chance to keep clear (rules 15 and 16).

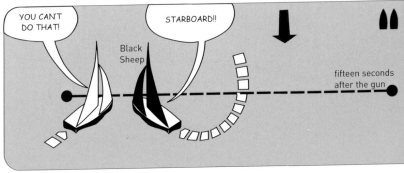

Black Sheep has changed course too quickly and not given the port tack boat room to keep clear. On this showing, Black Sheep's return to the fold would result in her having to do a Two-Turns Penalty.

When the race committee displays flag I as the preparatory signal, any boat whose hull, equipment or crew is on the course side of the starting line or its extensions during the minute before her starting signal must sail outside one end of the line, sail across the extension of the starting line from the course side to the pre-start side, and then start. She may not just dip back over the start line (rule 30.1).

Starting from the wrong side of the line

Cowboy enjoys right-of-way for two seconds more, then loses it as soon as the gun goes if she is caught with any part of the boat or crew on the wrong side of the line at the gun (rule 21.1). If she gets behind the line after the gun, she must not be in a position where the white boats cannot keep clear without having to anticipate Cowboy suddenly becoming the right-of-way boat (rule 15).

Overtaking to leeward

This is very common before and at the start, though the rules that apply are much the same as those that apply at any other time in the race.

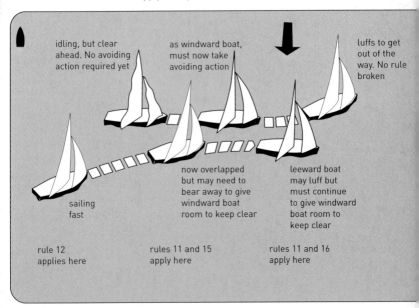

idling, but clear ahead. No avoiding action required yet

as windward boat, must now take avoiding action

luffs to get out of the way. No rule broken

now overlapped but may need to bear away to give windward boat room to keep clear

leeward boat may luff but must continue to give windward boat room to keep clear

sailing fast

rule 12 applies here

rules 11 and 15 apply here

rules 11 and 16 apply here

Moving backwards

A boat moving backwards (through the water) by backing a sail must keep clear of one that is not (rule 21.3).

WINDWARD LEG

A windward leg is one that a boat can complete only by putting in at least one tack.

OPPOSITE TACKS

this starboard tack boat has right-of-way over the port tack boat

ort tack

Port and starboard

A port tack boat must keep clear of a starboard tack boat (rule 10).

When a close-hauled starboard tack boat bears away to miss the port boat's stern and protests, and there is no collision, the port tack boat's helmsman must satisfy the protest committee that his boat would have kept clear had the starboard tack boat held her course (ISAF Case 50).

The right-of-way boat is required to avoid contact, but if there is no damage, the right-of-way boat cannot be penalized if she gave room to the port tack boat to keep clear. If there is damage which the right-of-way boat could have avoided (provided it is not serious) the right-of-way boat may do a Two-Turns Penalty to exonerate herself (rules 14 and 44.1).

port tack boat keeps clear

starboard tack

The keep-clear boat is, obviously, also required to try to avoid contact. If there is contact, provided there is no serious damage, the keep-clear boat may exonerate herself by taking a Two-Turns Penalty to cover the whole incident (rule 44.1). If either boat causes serious damage that she reasonably could have avoided, she must retire.

If the helmsman of a starboard tack boat doesn't want the port tack boat to tack on her lee bow, he may hail 'hold your course' and sail under her stern but the hail itself does not place any obligation on the port-tacker. The port tack boat may keep clear however she likes.

A starboard tack boat sailing downwind has right-of-way over a close-hauled port tack boat. But if the starboard tack boat changes course, she must give room to the port tack boat to keep clear (rules 10 and 16.1).

DON'T YOU KNOW ABOUT RULE 16?

STARBOARD!

Port and starboard when the starboard tack boat changes course

A port and starboard incident where the starboard tack boat changes course towards the port-tacker is quite different from the straightforward port and starboard case above. This situation is controlled by rule 16, which says that any right-of-way boat changing course must give the other boat room to keep clear.

The white boat on starboard is in the wrong because she changed course when the port boat was properly keeping clear, and gave no chance to the port-tacker to react to the new situation. Rule 16 doesn't stop the boat on starboard changing course when approaching a boat on port, provided there is room for the port tack boat to keep clear (rule 16.1).

Rule 16.1 can have the effect of preventing the starboard tack boat from taking advantage of a windshift. To use the windshift as a defence in a protest hearing, Black would have to satisfy the protest committee that the starboard tack boat's change of course gave her no opportunity to keep clear (rule 16.1).

wind shifts

wind 2 · wind 1

this starboard boat is lifted up on the windshift

here this port boat is clearly crossing the starboard boat

Port and starboard when the starboard tack boat has just tacked

'When a boat acquires right of way, she must initially give the other boat room to keep clear...' (rule 15)

If there was a protest, Jack-in-the-box would have to satisfy the protest committee that the tack was completed far enough from the other boat for her to be able to keep clear without having to anticipate the completion of Jack-in-the-box's tack.

Calling 'starboard'

There is no obligation to call 'starboard' when you are on starboard tack and a port tack boat is approaching, but it's often a good idea if you think he hasn't seen you. If there is an incident he might have to take a penalty, but you might lose a lot of time by getting tangled up with him.

The starboard tack boat on the right breaks no rule by hailing 'starboard', and then tacking.

A boat that hails 'starboard' when on port tack with the intention of intimidating an inexperienced skipper whose boat is on starboard tack would break the 'fair sailing' rule (rule 2 and ISAF Case 47).

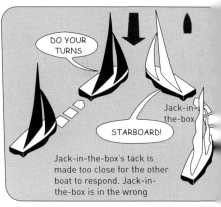

DO YOUR TURNS

Jack-in-the-box

STARBOARD!

Jack-in-the-box's tack is made too close for the other boat to respond. Jack-in-the-box is in the wrong

STARBOARD!

Opposite tack boat requiring room for an obstruction

There is, curiously, no way that a port tack boat that is prevented from tacking by an obstruction can legitimately force starboard tack boats to tack and give her room. Only when she is on the same tack can she hail for room. Here, the port and starboard rule (rule 10) applies, in spite of the fact that the port tack boat's only escape may be to bear away hard or go aground.

SAME TACK

Windward and leeward

When two boats on the same tack are close-hauled and overlapped, the windward boat must keep clear, even if the one to windward cannot sail as close to the wind as the leeward one (rule 11).

The leeward boat may not sail above her proper course (close-hauled here) unless she has luffing rights. She has luffing rights if she got into this over-lapped position by any way other than from clear astern (rules 11 and 17). If she luffs, she must give the windward boat room to keep clear (rule 16.1).

The crew or helmsman of the leeward boat may not deliberately reach out, sit out or trapeze with the intention of hitting the windward boat. This would be penalized under the fair sailing rule (rule 2 and ISAF Case 73).

Luffing

The black boat got her overlap by tacking into this position so she has the right to luff, right up to head-to-wind.

However, while she was tacking she was the keep-clear boat, and she has tacked into a right-of-way position, so she has to initially give the other boat room to keep clear (rule 15).

Then she may luff. If she does, she must give the white boat room to keep clear (rule 16.1).

The white boat must keep clear (rule 11).

Both boats must try to avoid contact (rule 14).

Bearing away

Provided the leeward boat isn't made to change course to avoid hitting the windward boat, the windward boat may bear away below close-hauled as White does here. But as windward boat she must keep clear (rule 11).

If the leeward boat has luffing rights (the right to sail above her proper course), she can luff at any time, but if she does, she must give the windward boat room to keep clear (rule 16.1).

Calling for room at a continuing obstruction

If Mud Tickler carries on she'll hit the shore; if she tacks she'll hit the white boat. The rules provide a way out of this dilemma provided both boats are on the same tack and Mud Tickler is close-hauled (or above): Mud Tickler can hail 'room to tack', or something similar at the white boat.

The white boat must respond immediately either by:

1 tacking as soon as possible or

2 hailing 'you tack' (rule 20.1(b)).

If the white boat chooses to tack, Mud Tickler must tack as soon as possible (rule 20.1(c)).

White may prefer to let Mud Tickler tack, keep out of her way and really squeeze into the shore herself. Then White must call 'you tack' and avoid Mud Tickler.

As soon as White has made her 'you tack' call, Mud Tickler must tack as soon as possible (rule 20(b) and (c)).

Problems can arise when 'short tacking' against a tidal stream. Whether the outside boat has the obligation to tack hinges on how far apart the boats are when the inside boat needs to tack. There is no set number of boat lengths – the distance will vary according to the conditions and the type of boat – but the criteria for deciding are quite clear. The outside boat is not required to change course when:

1 the inside boat can tack out from the shore and back again on to her original tack without any risk of forcing the outside boat to change course or

2 the inside boat can tack and bear away behind the outside boat without difficulty.

If White is able to tack out from the shore and back on to her original tack without Black being forced to alter course to keep clear, then Black need not alter course. Black must, however, still respond to the hail by hailing 'you tack'. Here White was forced to fall back on to starboard tack before getting to close-hauled on port tack. Black did not give room and must do a Two-Turns Penalty (rule 20).

In this sequence (right), Black took a chance by hailing 'you tack' but, as it turned out, White was able to tack and bear away behind Black without difficulty, so there was no rule broken (rule 20).

Calling for room at a non-continuing obstruction that is not a mark

A non-continuing obstruction is one that can be passed on either side and requires a boat not less than a length away to make a substantial change of course to miss it. Moored boats, minuscule islands, capsized boats, a right-of-way boat, may all be non-continuing obstructions (the definition is on page 24).

Once the 'room to tack' call has been made here by Black, White must respond exactly as in the section above (rule 20). The fact that White would have missed the obstruction anyway doesn't matter, she must respond. Nor does it matter that Black chose to tack rather than bear away and go to leeward of the obstruction. There is no rule that dictates that a boat should take the shortest route around an obstruction. Although if Black needed to make only a small change of course when one length away, the rules don't allow her to call for water to tack: she must then make the course change, staying on the same tack (Definition of Obstruction).

A starboard tack boat as an obstruction

One of the most common obstructions to a close-hauled boat on port tack is a boat on starboard tack.

Stool-pigeon is entitled to hail for room to tack, and the white boat must either tack immediately or call 'you tack' and give room. Stool-pigeon has to see this situation coming in good time or she'll be too late to call and won't be able to get out of the starboard-tacker's way (rule 20 and Definition of Obstruction).

When Stool-pigeon calls clearly for room to tack, in good time, and White fails to respond, the responsibility is entirely White's and no blame falls on Stool-pigeon for White's failure to tack. However, if there is no response to the first hail, Stool-pigeon must hail again more loudly (ISAF Cases 3 and 54).

Instead of tacking, Stool-pigeon can choose to bear away astern of the starboard boat, since an obstruction can be taken on either side, but she must then give enough room to White if she wishes to go underneath (rule 19.2(b) and Definition of Obstruction).

If White asks for water to bear away behind the starboard boat at the same moment as Stool-pigeon asks for room to tack, Stool-pigeon's call governs. White gets room only if Stool-pigeon chooses not to hail for room to tack, in which case Stool-pigeon must give room whether or not White asks for it (Section C preamble and 20).

 ## Forcing another boat to overstand a weather mark

The team racing ploy of forcing an opponent on the same tack to sail beyond the lay line and overstand the weather mark is explained on page 68.

TACKING

Tacking ahead of another boat

A boat that is tacking is required to keep clear of other boats until she is on a close-hauled course (rule 13).

Even when the tacking boat has completed her tack she is not necessarily in the clear. She mustn't tack into a right-of-way position (for example, clear ahead) if the other boat cannot keep clear without having to anticipate that she'll be there. So if the other boat cannot keep clear without having to begin to change course starting from the moment the tacking boat is on a close-hauled course, the tacking boat has broken the rule (rule 15). In the situation (above) the tacking boat has clearly broken a rule (13 or 15).

In the situation below, White becomes the right-of-way boat when she is on a close-hauled course. Black was able to keep clear without having to anticipate, and she kept clear, so no rule was broken.

Tacking in the water of a port tack boat

It is not possible to tack as close to another boat when going from starboard tack to port as it is when going from port to starboard.

the port boat bears away to go behind the starboard boat

the tack is completed but the other boat has been forced to alter course to avoid the collision

the starboard boat decides to tack – too late

While White is luffing up to head-to-wind, she is on starboard tack. As she is changing course she is required to give room to Black to keep clear (rule 16.1). In this picture Black can easily keep clear by luffing. If White passes through head-to-wind, she becomes the keep-clear boat and remains the keep-clear boat until she is close-hauled on the new tack (rule 13).

When the port-tack boat is sailing a course to pass astern of the starboard-tack boat, if the starboard-tack boat (White) changes course, the port-tack boat (Black) must be able to keep clear without having to alter course immediately to keep clear (rule 16.2).

at this moment the port boat is required to begin avoiding action

the tack is completed

the port boat bears away to go behind the starboard boat

the starboard boat decides to tack

White could cross ahead of Black and Black must keep clear. But White might have a tactical reason for wanting to be on port tack, and want to encourage Black to tack.

At the moment White's tack is completed, Black must take whatever avoiding action is necessary to avoid White. By tacking ahead or to windward of Black, Black will be encouraged to tack as Black will not want to sail close astern of White, or in her wind shadow. However, if Black is forced to avoid White by starting to keep clear before White has completed her tack, White will have broken rule 13. In practice, if Black thinks White has not broken rule 13, she will luff and tack before White's tack is complete so as not to spend any time in White's bad air.

Simultaneous tacking

When two boats are tacking at the same time, the one on the other's port side keeps clear (rule 13). However, until they pass head-to-wind, they are on their original tacks. Once they are both through head-to-wind, then whoever is on the right is in the right.

As long as both boats are between head-to-wind and close-hauled, then the one on the other's port side must keep clear. In dinghies and small keel-boats it can be risky to tack immediately after crossing close ahead of a port tack boat – especially if the port tack boat has borne away to miss the starboard-tacker's stern, since she'll be moving extra fast during a tack.

MARK ROUNDING

The mark-rounding rules come into effect when a boat reaches the 'zone' (normally three hull-lengths from the mark), and continue until the mark is left astern.

Where the mark-rounding rules come into force

There are special rules that apply to passing or rounding marks and obstructions (rules 18 and 19). This section is about passing or rounding marks; passing obstructions is dealt with in the sections on windward legs and downwind legs.

The mark-rounding rules come into force when a boat enters the 'zone' and ceases to have any effect when Mark-Room is no longer needed – that is, the mark has been left astern on the new leg with no danger of hitting it (preamble to Section C).

The 'zone' is the area around a mark within a distance of three hull lengths of the boat nearer to it. This is often referred to as 'the circle', but in fact it's an arc for the approaching boats, not those who are saying goodbye to the mark. The sailing instructions may change to 'two' or 'four' the number of hull lengths determining the zone around the marks, provided that the number is the same for all boats using those marks (rule 86.1(b) and Definition of Zone).

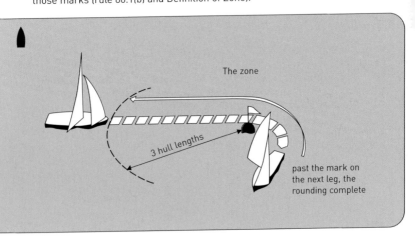

The zone

3 hull lengths

past the mark on the next leg, the rounding complete

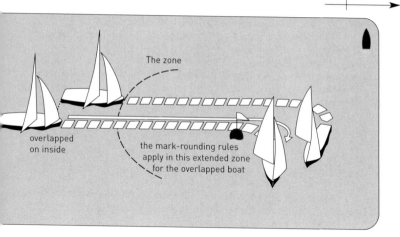

The zone

overlapped
on inside

the mark-rounding rules
apply in this extended zone
for the overlapped boat

The most usual case where the area in which the mark-rounding rules must be considered even though they don't yet apply (because the boats are further away than three lengths) is when several boats are overlapped and the outside boats are required to give Mark-Room as soon as one of them enters the zone which may mean having to start giving room well before the zone.

The penalty for touching a mark

A boat touches a mark when any part of her hull, crew or equipment touches it. So a neat hand-off or a spinnaker sheet touching a flag on the mark is a touch. The mark's mooring line or chain is not counted as part of the mark (Definition of Mark).

A boat is exonerated for hitting a mark if she sails well clear of all other boats as soon as possible and remains clear while making a turn, including a tack and a gybe (or a gybe and a tack) (rule 44).

When a boat hits the 'wrong' side of a mark (sails the wrong side of it and hits it) she must go off and do her turn, and then come back and round it on the right side. If, however, there are no other boats about, and she can do her turn round the mark without getting in anyone's way, she fulfils both requirements in one move.

If a boat has gained a significant advantage in the race or series by touching a mark, she must retire (rule 44.1(b)).

Forced on to a mark by another boat

When a boat is forced on to a mark by another boat that has broken a rule, the mark-hitter need not take a penalty. If there is a protest (eg by the mark-hitter or the wrong-doer) and the wrong-doer is penalized (whether or not it was the boat that was protested), then the mark-hitter will be exonerated.

If a boat hits a mark, and breaks a 'when boats meet' rule, (for example because she takes room to which she is not entitled) she can be exonerated from both breaches by doing just one Two-Turns Penalty. However, if she gained a significant advantage, she must retire (rule 44.1(b)).

In the rare event of a mark being submerged by a boat sailing over it, then shooting out of the water to hit a following boat, this boat need not take a penalty. She can't protest against the mark, but she can protest against the boat that caused its irregular behaviour. However, she is still obliged to go to the correct side of it, no matter where it surfaces.

Rights and obligations of a boat that has just hit a mark

A boat that misjudges her mark-rounding and makes contact with the mark must begin to get well clear of other boats as soon as possible, and then promptly make one turn including one tack and one gybe. She retains all her normal rights until she is well clear of other boats. If she is taking the penalty at the finishing line and she is on the post-finish side of the line after doing the turn, she must return completely to the course side of the line before finishing.

If she has gained a significant advantage in the race or series by touching the mark, the option of taking a penalty is not open to her and she must retire, even if taking the penalty would set her back more than she'd gained (rule 44.1(b)).

Rounding a mark in the wrong direction

After rounding a mark the wrong way, the mistake can be corrected by unwinding. To do this correctly, a string representing the boat's track must, when drawn tight, lie on the required side of the mark (rule 28.1). You don't lose any rights, just because you're going back to unwind or are in the process of unwinding.

mark to be left to port

rounds the wrong way

corrects the mistake

A mark is only a mark of the course for the leg

A mark is only a mark of the course for a particular boat when it begins, bounds or ends the leg of the course on which that boat is sailing (rule 28.2). So on the leg from mark 3 to mark 4, mark 1 can be hit without penalty, and between a boat rounding mark 1 on her way to mark 2, and a boat coming down from mark 3 to mark 4, the boat rounding has no right to 'Mark-Room' because they are not both rounding the mark (rule 18.1).

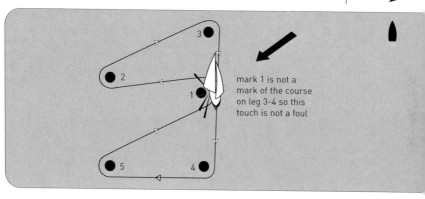

mark 1 is not a
mark of the course
on leg 3-4 so this
touch is not a foul

Mark missing or moved

The race committee should return a drift-ing mark to its stated position if possible. If that isn't possible they must replace it by a new one with 'similar characteristics' or a buoy or boat displaying code flag 'M' and make repetitive sounds (rule 34).

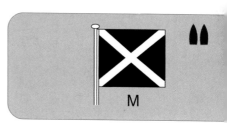

M

ROUNDING AT THE END OF A DOWNWIND LEG

Room at a mark

A windward boat that is overlapped with others outside her has the right to Mark-Room, provided the overlap is established before the leading boat enters the 'zone' (normally three hull lengths of the boat near-est to the mark) and in addition provided that if the overlap is established from clear astern, the outside boat is able to give room (rule 18.2(e)). The explanation of an overlap is on page 23.

If the leading boat is unable to give Mark-Room when the overlap is first established from clear astern, the inside boat is not enti-tled to it (rule 18.2(e)). In other words she

wind

The zone

can't expect an outside boat to do the impossible. This can happen where a group of boats are in line abreast and cannot shift aside fast enough to accommodate a late inside overlapper. When boats are planing in at high speed, it is often impossible for an outside boat to give room when the overlap is established close to the zone.

If there is doubt as to whether the inside boat that was clear astern established the overlap in time (either in time for the outside boat to be able to give Mark-Room, or before the first of the boats reached the zone) then they must assume the boat claiming Mark-Room is not entitled to it. Circumstances where a helmsman is unable to give Mark-Room because he isn't properly in control of his boat are not included: a helmsman's incompetence or inexperience is no defence.

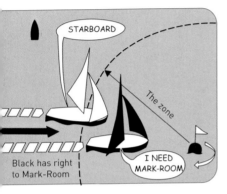

Port and starboard at a downwind mark

When one of the boats enters the zone, the Mark-Room rules apply (rule 18).

Here the black boat on port tack is on the inside. She had an inside overlap when the leading boat reached the zone. White must give her room to sail to the mark, and then give room to sail her proper course while at the mark, so here White must give Black room to gybe (rule 18.2 and Definition of Mark-Room).

When there is doubt about a late overlap

When there is reasonable doubt as to whether a boat, that comes from clear astern claiming to have established the inside overlap, has established it in time, then the boats must presume she has not (rule 18.2(d)).

Pusher would find it very difficult to establish that her inside overlap was made soon enough. A witness in another boat or ashore might clinch it, but even so, Pusher would be foolish in this situation to round on the inside and risk being protested. Because of the 'when there is reasonable doubt' rule, Pusher doesn't have the right to Mark-Room. If the outside boat indicates his acceptance that Pusher has established the overlap in time, then that's a different matter; Pusher would be entitled to pass inside (rule 18.2(d)).

When there is doubt that an overlap has been broken

Here, two overlapped boats are approaching a mark and just before entering the zone, the outside boat claims that the overlap has been broken. But if there is 'reasonable doubt', then the boats must presume the overlap still exists and the inside boat has the right to Mark-Room (rule 18.2(d)).

If the inside boat disputes a marginal 'clear ahead' claim, the outside boat would be stupid to try and push her luck by denying room to the inside boat.

Quicksilver would be hard pushed to win a protest if she didn't give room at the mark, but if she can stay ahead of Barnacle Bill, until the mark is astern of BB, then she will have fulfilled her obligations to give Mark-Room (rule 18.2).

Hailing for room

The rules don't require a hail, but a hail that there is or isn't an overlap, made well before the zone, often avoids disagreement and panic when it comes to who should be doing what at the mark.

How overlaps operate when boats are making a wide rounding

In a big fleet it often happens at a leeward mark that boats round very wide at the end of a downwind leg so that they come in close to the mark. If a boat goes so wide that she enters the zone at right angles to the oncoming fleet, the whole fleet is entitled to Mark-Room – they are forward of the line at right angles to her aftermost point. They won't all be able to make use of their right to Mark-Room, but some might be able to, as Interloper might be able to do here.

because of this boat's angle of approach, Interloper is entitled to Mark-Room

Losing the right to Mark-Room when a boat is carried past a mark by a current or tidal stream

A boat with the right to Mark-Room that enters the zone and leaves it has to re-establish her rights when she re-enters the zone.

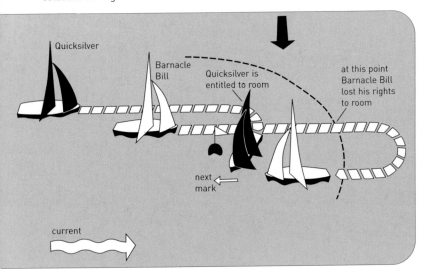

The same principle applies in really windy conditions when a skipper chooses to tack round instead of gybing and during his tack sails past the mark and outside the zone. He must establish new rights on re-entering the zone.

How much room must the outside boat give?

If the outside boat is the keep-clear boat (because she is on the same tack as the inside boat and is to windward, or on opposite tacks and she is on port tack) then she must keep clear, and the inside boat may sail the course she would have sailed in the absence of the outside boat (her 'proper course'). Furthermore, if the boats are on the same tack, and the inside boat is to leeward, and the inside boat established the overlap in any other way than from clear astern, and her proper course at the mark does not include a gybe, then she may sail straight ahead, or luff at any time during the rounding of the mark, right up to head-to-wind, provided she luffs in such a way that she gives room to the windward boat to keep clear.

If the boat required to give room is the right-of-way boat then she must give 'Mark-Room' which is room for the inside boat (or boat ahead) to sail to the mark, and then sail her proper course while at the mark. However, Mark-Room does not include room to tack unless the boat is overlapped to windward and on the inside of the boat required to give Mark-Room (rule 18.2 and Definition of Mark-Room).

More room is needed in rough weather. Although an inexperienced helmsman cannot count on any extra space to allow for his lack of skill, any doubt in a protest will usually go in favour of the inside boat.

White's rounding here, in which she sails wide for purely tactical reasons, breaks rule 11 (windward boat to keep clear). The dividing line between what is a 'seamanlike' rounding and a rounding made primarily for maximum tactical gain can be a fine one. If there's a protest, the outside boat will need to satisfy the protest committee that she gave sufficient room, and the inside boat failed to keep clear. In this situation Black would win the protest. One and a half lengths given by Black was plenty of room and White failed to keep clear.

this boat is 1½ lengths from the mark solely for tactical reasons – this is too wide in moderate weather

The zone

inside boat has right to Mark-Room only while passing the mark

next mark

as soon as the mark is passed, this boat should be keeping clear – a Two-Turns Penalty is required

this right-of-way boat has luffed, giving room to the windward boat to keep clear

The mark is passed when it is left astern with no chance of colliding with it. When the mark is passed, the inside boat's right to Mark-Room expires (ISAF Case 25).

Breaking an overlap inside the zone

An outside boat that is required to give Mark-Room because there was an overlap before the first boat entered the zone must continue to give Mark-Room if she becomes clear ahead inside the zone (rule 18.2(c)).

overlapped going into the zone

The zone

mark

overlap broken

Quicksilver

Barnacle Bill

Quicksilver must still give room and will be penalized if Barnacle Bill has to alter course to avoid her

Go-Getter

Go-Getter's
proper course

When the inside boat needs to gybe round a mark

When the inside right-of-way boat's proper course includes a gybe then until she gybes she must take no more room than that required to sail a proper course, even though she is the right-of-way boat (rule 18.4).

The windward boat must keep clear (rule 11).

Even if Go-Getter has luffing rights (because the windward boat established the overlap to windward of her), when they're in the zone, Go-Getter must not sail further from the mark than necessary to sail her proper course (rule 18.4). The windward boat must keep clear (rule 11).

This does not apply at a gate mark (see page 68).

When the inside boat has luffing rights and there is a proper course she can sail without gybing

When the inside boat, of two overlapping boats, did not get her overlap from clear astern (so she has luffing rights), and there is a proper course she can sail without gybing, then she may sail straight past the mark, or luff at any time if she gives room to the windward boat to keep clear (rule 11).

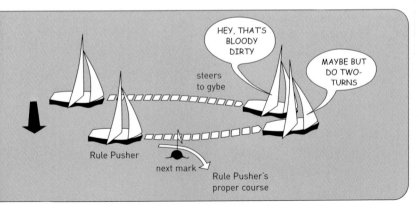

steers to gybe

HEY, THAT'S BLOODY DIRTY

MAYBE BUT DO TWO-TURNS

Rule Pusher

next mark

Rule Pusher's proper course

Forcing another boat to the wrong side of a mark

Luffing another boat the wrong side of a mark is rarely wise in normal fleet racing but is a legitimate tactic to break an overlap, or if near the end of a series you need to stop a rival getting a good finishing position to enhance your overall score compared to his.

For a leeward boat to be allowed to luff a windward boat to the wrong side of the mark, the leeward boat must have luffing rights, and neither boat must be in the zone. If in a protest hearing there was a doubt whether one of them had reached the zone, then the protest committee may give the windward boat the benefit of the doubt.

If, during the luffing process, either boat enters the zone, then the leeward boat must immediately bear away to round the mark and, if the windward boat is inside, give Mark-Room.

No hail is required, though it is often worthwhile in order to avoid contact (rules 16.1, 11, 17 and 14).

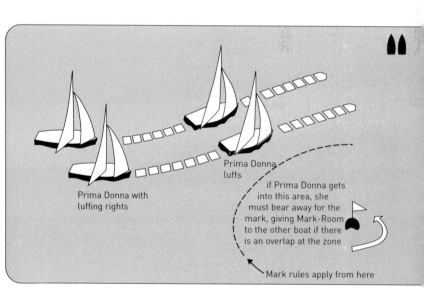

Prima Donna luffs

Prima Donna with luffing rights

if Prima Donna gets into this area, she must bear away for the mark, giving Mark-Room to the other boat if there is an overlap at the zone

Mark rules apply from here

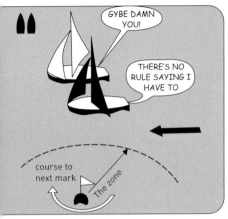

Using starboard rights to sail a boat the wrong side of a mark

When two boats are on opposite tacks the starboard boat may sail any course and the port boat must keep clear (rule 10 and ISAF Case 9). This means that provided both boats remain outside the zone, the starboard tack boat may take the port boat the wrong side of the mark. No hail is necessary but if the starboard tack boat changes course, she must give the port tack boat room to keep clear (rules 10 and 16).

Passing a mark in opposite directions

When a mark does not have a required side for both boats then the 'mark rounding' rules do not apply; the normal 'when boats meet' rules apply instead.

ROUNDING AT THE END OF A WINDWARD LEG

On opposite tacks – port and starboard

When boats on opposite tacks are at a windward mark, the rules apply essentially as though the mark wasn't there (rules 18.1(b) and 10).

A starboard tack boat can sail in a straight line beyond the mark perfectly legitimately to put a port tack boat about (ISAF Case 9).

The rule that says a right-of-way boat changing course must give the keep-clear boat room to keep clear, applies in a port-and-starboard situation at the mark (rule 16.1).

The mark-rounding rules do not apply between a boat approaching a mark and one leaving it. Here, if White bears away any more she will break the rule that says if a right of way boat changes course she must give room to the other boat to keep clear. Black is sailing a course which keeps clear and does not have to anticipate that White wants to gybe or turn down onto a run (rules 16.1 and 18.1(c)).

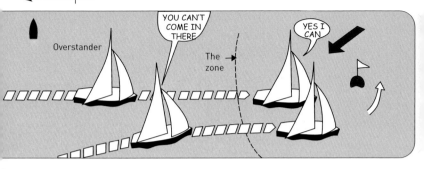

Outside the zone, Overstander is required to keep clear as windward boat (rule 11). But as soon as the leading boat reaches the zone, the rules that apply to marks come into play. If Overstander has an overlap when the leading boat reaches the zone, then the leeward boat must give Overstander room to sail directly to the mark and then her proper course round the mark (rule 18.2(b) and Definition of Mark-Room).

Overstander does not have the right to bear away to be able to come up tight on the mark, even if she reasonably believes that is her proper course.

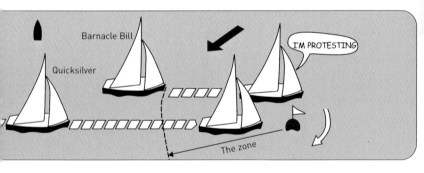

Barnacle Bill is clear ahead on entering the zone so at the mark Quicksilver must give her Mark-Room even if she later gets an inside overlap. In the zone it is irrelevant that Barnacle Bill becomes the windward boat here because even if she breaks rule 11 when she is rounding the mark (taking the Mark-Room to which she is entitled), she will be exonerated for the breach (rule 18.5).

When boats are overlapped on entering the zone, an inside leeward boat below the lay line may luff to round the mark because, even without the right to sail above her proper course (because she established the overlap from clear astern), to luff above close-hauled may be her proper course round the mark (Definition of Mark-Room).

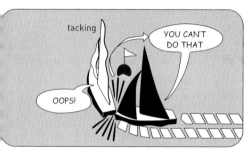

When both boats approach a mark on the same track with one clear ahead of the other on entering the zone, the boat ahead may luff to head-to-wind at the mark, but must keep clear from the moment she passes head-to-wind to the moment she is close-hauled on the new tack. If she tacks on to port tack, and the other boat is still on starboard tack, she'll have to continue to keep clear (rules 13 and 10). The boat that was clear astern may luff to prevent the boat ahead from tacking, provided she keeps clear of her until the boat that was clear ahead passes head to wind.

A leading boat that enters the zone clear ahead may slow down, forcing the boat to sail outside. The boat now on the outside must continue to give Mark-Room. Foiler does nothing wrong here. She is entitled to slow down, and when Thruster gets an outside overlap she must continue to give Foiler Mark-Room, including room to tack (rule 18.2(b) and Definition of Mark-Room).

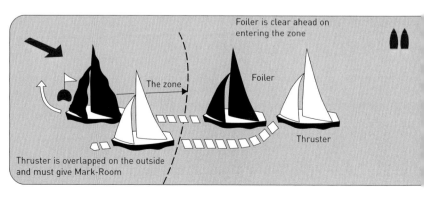

Tacking within the zone

Risktaker completes her tack inside the zone. While she was on port tack she had to keep clear of Speedy approaching on starboard tack. When Risktaker passed head-to-wind, she changed tack, and she was probably clear ahead, but rule 13 says she must keep clear until she is close-hauled. Now, to add to her worries, if Speedy gets an overlap to leeward at any time during the rounding, Risktaker must give Mark-Room (and Speedy can sail her proper course around the mark). And Risktaker must not force Speedy above close-hauled to avoid contact (rule 18.3). Furthermore, Risktaker has no protection from rule 15 which normally requires a boat that establishes right-of-way (for example by getting an overlap to leeward) to initially give the other boat room to clear.

Risktaker

Speedy

The zone

White's tack is completed inside the zone so Black is entitled to sail her proper course around the mark and White must keep clear

A special case of room to tack when the windward mark is big

This covers the unusual case where the windward mark is also an obstruction.

If White cannot fetch the mark (pass it without tacking) then she must respond to the hail by either:

1 tacking immediately
2 hailing 'you tack' and give room for the black boat to tack and avoid her.

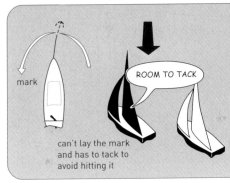

ROOM TO TACK

mark

can't lay the mark and has to tack to avoid hitting it

If she tacks, no rules have been broken and there are no grounds for protest.

If White thinks she can lay the mark without tacking (she may luff and squeeze round, provided she doesn't pass head-to-wind), she still needs to respond to Black's hail, but she would then be justified in protesting Black (rule 20.3).

Black should hail early enough to leave room to escape in case White chooses to try to lay the mark; if Black hits the mark and White succeeds in laying it, Black must do a One-Turn Penalty; if Black hits the mark and White fails to lay it, Black may sail on, and may protest White if she doesn't retire or take a penalty.

A special case on a port hand rounding

Both Complacent and Ricochet must keep clear of Starboard under rule 10 while on port tack and under rule 13 while tacking. Ricochet should have acted sooner by hailing Complacent for room to tack to keep clear of Starboard (or bearing away to pass astern of Starboard, in which case Ricochet, as the outside boat under rule 19.2(b), was required to give Complacent, the inside overlapping boat, room to do the same). In the situation shown, Ricochet has left it too late to do that. If, in responding to Ricochet's hail, Complacent collides with the mark, Ricochet will be in the wrong for forcing another boat to break a rule. If Ricochet doesn't do a Two-Turns Penalty, Complacent may protest (rule 20.1(a)).

STARBOARD

Complacent

WATER TO TACK

Ricochet

Sailing another boat past a mark

This is a manoeuvre used in team racing and, accidentally, by beginners in fleet racing.

If they are team racing, there is no rule to stop Manipulator sailing as far beyond the weather mark as she likes, forcing Victim to overstand and letting Opportunist round ahead (ISAF Case 15). Manipulator and Opportunist would be team mates and Victim would be pushed behind Opportunist. Victim is, however, the right-of-way boat. Manipulator must keep clear, even if Victim luffs. If Victim luffs she must give room to Manipulator to keep clear (rules 11 and 16.1). In fleet racing, Manipulator's actions would have to be consistent with achieving her best finishing position in the race or series (rule 2).

Gate marks

Many courses nowadays include a 'gate' consisting of two marks about 6 hull-lengths apart placed at right angles to the wind direction, usually at the leeward end of a leg. Boats can choose which mark to round provided they sail between the marks. At a gate mark the inside right-of-way boat with luffing rights need not gybe (rules 18.4 and 28.1).

This gate is at the leeward end of a leg. If this were not a gate then *Runaway Child* must gybe to sail her proper course but at a gate, if she has luffing rights, she can delay her gybe or sail to the other gate mark.

DOWNWIND LEG

When boats are running
or reaching.

OPPOSITE TACKS

Port and starboard

A boat on port tack must keep clear of a boat on starboard tack (rule 10). This is a basic right-of-way rule.

starboard tack boat has right-of-way

this boat is on port tack and must keep clear

The starboard tack boat may sail towards the port tack boat (her 'proper course' is irrelevant) but if she changes course she must give the port tack boat room to keep clear (rule 16.1).

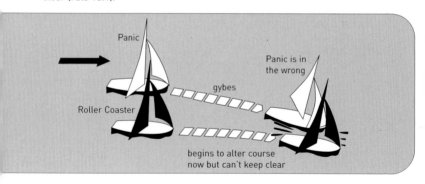

Panic

Panic is in the wrong

gybes

Roller Coaster

begins to alter course now but can't keep clear

When a keep-clear boat does something to become a right-of-way boat, she must initially give the other boat room to keep clear. In the first position, Panic is the keep-clear windward boat, required to keep clear (rule 11). She decides to gybe, and becomes the right-of-way boat on starboard tack. Roller Coaster must keep clear (rule 10) but Panic must initially give room to her to keep clear (rule 15). If Panic doesn't do a Two-Turns Penalty, a protest by Roller Coaster is likely to succeed. Had Panic been on starboard tack all along, and made the change of course shown in the diagram, Roller Coaster would be in the wrong (rule 10). The starboard tack boat is allowed to sail any course she likes provided that if she changes course, she gives 'room to keep clear' to the port tack boat (rules 10 and 16.1).

Not overlapped

In open water the port and starboard rule (rule 10) applies even when boats are not overlapped. The rule that requires that a boat clear astern keeps clear of a boat ahead (rule 12) applies only when both boats are on the same tack.

White thinks that because Black is clear astern, Black should keep clear, but in this case the white boat is wrong and must do a Two-Turns Penalty (rule 10). However, if there is damage, the black boat will also have to do a penalty. She should have avoided contact (rule 14).

Room to pass a continuing obstruction

The normal basic rules apply between two boats passing a continuing obstruction such as a shoreline (if on the same tack, clear-astern keeps clear of clear-ahead, windward keeps clear of leeward). However, a keep-clear boat is entitled to room on the inside if at the time she gets the overlap there is room for her to pass between the right-of-way boat and the obstruction (rule 19.2(c)).

Room at an obstruction which is not continuing

The same as for 'Downwind Same Tack' (page 75).

SAME TACK

 ### Windward boat keeps clear
A windward boat is required to keep clear of a leeward boat (rule 11).

In open water (away from marks and obstructions) a windward boat must keep clear of a boat to leeward. When the leeward boat becomes overlapped from astern within two of her hull-lengths, she mustn't sail above her proper course (explained on page 25) while they are overlapped, on the same tack and the distance between them is less than two lengths (unless in doing so she promptly sails astern of the other boat); but even if she does sail above her proper course (breaking rule 17) the windward boat must still keep clear (rule 11).

Overtaking another boat
Because they are on the same tack, the boat clear astern is required to keep clear (rule 12).

More often the overtaking boat doesn't follow exactly in the wake of the boat ahead, but becomes overlapped to leeward.

transition period as windward/leeward rights take over from clear ahead/clear astern rights

windward boat has to keep clear (rule 11)

windward boat

leeward boat

clear astern, has to keep clear (rule 12)

now overlapped, so windward boat must keep clear, but she must be given room to do so (rule 15)

leeward boat may not sail above her proper course (rule 17)

The obligation on the boat astern to keep clear switches off as the overlap is established. The windward/leeward rule then takes over and the windward boat is required to begin any necessary avoiding action, but the leeward boat must initially give her room to keep clear and in addition must not sail above her proper course. The windward boat may well have to sail above her own proper course to fulfil her obligation to keep clear (rules 12, 11, 15, 17 and ISAF Case 14).

Overtaking more than one boat

A boat clear astern wanting to sail between two overlapped boats ahead needs to consider these factors: the boat to leeward will remain the right-of-way boat and may luff, and the boat to windward has to luff to keep clear only after the boat astern gets an overlap. Chancer may be heading for trouble. If the windward boat cannot give room from the time the overlap began then Chancer has no right to room. Even if the leeward boat does not have luffing rights with respect to the windward boat, her proper course may be to luff to avoid the disturbed air from Chancer (rule 19.2(b)).

Chancer

the windward boat must keep clear

windward boat

leeward boat

leeward boat may not sail above her proper course unless she has luffing rights over the windward boat (rule 17)

Black may sail into the gap and when she becomes overlapped with the windward boat, the windward boat must keep clear. The leeward boat may luff but must give room for the boats to windward to keep clear (rule 19.2(b), Definition of Obstruction, and ISAF Case 29).

Assuming that Prudence established her overlap to leeward of the windward boat from clear astern, she must sail no higher than her proper course. But her proper course is to sail to windward of the boat ahead so she may sail that course

windward boat must keep clear of Prudence (rule 11)

windward boat must continue to keep clear

Prudence – not overlapped on the leeward boat

Prudence

leeward boat

and the windward boat must keep clear. It would be just the same as if the leeward boat was a small island or an obstacle in the water. They are all 'non-continuing obstructions' (rule 19.2(b) and Definition of Obstruction).

Room to pass a continuing obstruction

A boat clear astern that is required to keep clear is entitled to room to sail into a gap between a boat ahead and a continuing obstruction, such as a shoreline, only when, at the moment the overlap is first established, there is enough room for her to sail through the gap (rule 19.2(c)).

this boat is entitled to room between the other boat and the shore because there was room for her to sail through the gap when she first established the overlap (rule 19.2(c))

shoreline

this boat is the right-of-way boat but must give room because the inside boat gained a legitimate overlap (rule 19.2(c))

this boat may go either side

rock

this boat must give room if necessary

Room at an obstruction that is not continuing

When overlapping boats approach a non-continuing obstruction, if the leeward boat has luffing rights she can pass on either side and the windward boat must keep clear. If the leeward boat does not have luffing rights then she can go to windward only if that is a proper course for her. In this diagram it is too late for White to go to windward of the island so she must give room to Black if Black chooses to go to leeward.

If the boats become overlapped near the obstruction, the inside boat is entitled to room only if the outside boat has been able to give room from the time the overlap began (rule 19.2(b)).

Luffing rights – two-boat situations

When boats become overlapped in any way other than the leeward boat establishing the overlap from clear astern within two lengths of her hull (laterally), the leeward boat has what is colloquially called 'luffing rights'. In other words, the right to sail above her proper course. A leeward boat with luffing rights may luff right up to head-to-wind (if she goes any further she will change tacks and no longer be the leeward boat).

However, there is one onerous restriction on the leeward boat: she must give room to the windward boat to keep clear. She may not luff so quickly that the windward boat is unable to respond to keep clear.

The windward boat must keep clear. In practice this means that whenever there are converging courses and a risk of collision, the windward boat must respond promptly by changing course so that they are no longer on a collision course.

this boat must respond properly

Black has the right to sail above her proper course

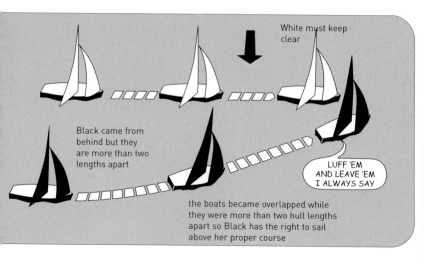

White must keep clear

Black came from behind but they are more than two lengths apart

LUFF 'EM AND LEAVE 'EM I ALWAYS SAY

the boats became overlapped while they were more than two hull lengths apart so Black has the right to sail above her proper course

she now has
luffing rights

she gybes

Here the black boat gybes, and becomes the right-of-way boat with luffing rights (the right to sail above her proper course). When she becomes the right-of-way boat, she must initially give White room to keep clear even if she doesn't change course, then she may luff but, if she does, she must give White room to keep clear (rules 15 and 16.1).

Luffing several boats

In the next picture, the first position shows L and I on opposite tacks. Boat I can sail any course but if she bears away she must give L room to keep clear, and of course Boat I is clear astern of W so must keep clear of her. L then gybes and since she did not establish the overlap on I from clear astern, L has luffing rights over I. L may sail higher than her proper course but must give room to I to keep clear. Now boat I gets an overlap to leeward of W. According to the definition of overlap (see page 21), L is overlapped to leeward of W too (since I is between W and L), and the overlap was established to leeward of W, so at the moment I is overlapped with W, L loses her luffing rights and must bear away to a course no higher than her proper course.

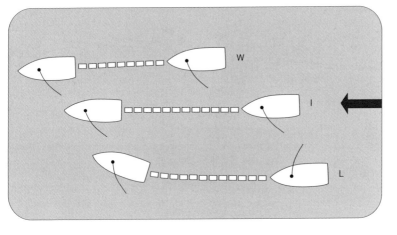

W

I

L

Stopping a luff

This sequence shows how a boat with luffing rights loses those rights. Soon after position 1, L and W become overlapped. As L didn't establish the overlap from clear astern L has luffing rights. W's wind-shadow affects L and W gains on L. At position 3, L luffs giving room to W to keep clear, and W responds. A sharp luff by W at position 4 breaks the overlap. L is now clear astern and becomes the keep-clear boat. W bears away and a new overlap is established. This time L establishes the overlap from clear astern so she doesn't have luffing rights, and she must sail no higher than her proper course. Her proper course is the course she would sail in the absence of W, starting from where she is at that moment, to finish as soon as possible. This means she will have to bear away at position 5. If she doesn't, W might want to protest, but she must still keep clear (rules 11, 12, 16.1 and 17).

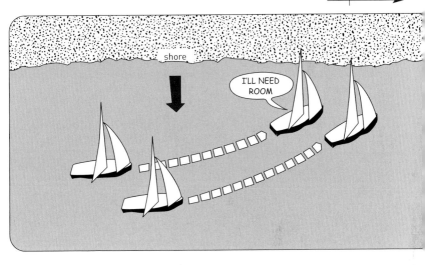

If the windward boat needs room because of a continuing obstruction such as the shore, then the leeward boat must give room. If there is something preventing the windward boat from responding to the luff, then the leeward boat must not luff. There is no requirement for the inside boat to hail, but it's a good idea (rule 19.2(c)).

Sailing above a proper course

When two boats are overlapped, and the leeward boat established the overlap from clear astern and less than two of her hull lengths, the leeward boat may not sail above her proper course while she remains overlapped on the same tack and within two lengths (rule 17).

But when the windward boat protests, claiming that the leeward boat is sailing above her proper course, the protest committee will not penalize the leeward boat unless it is satisfied the course was not a course that could reasonably be described as 'a course she would sail to finish as soon as possible in the absence of the windward boat' (Definition of Proper Course and ISAF Case 14).

When the leeward boat has to gybe to fulfil her obligation not to sail above her proper course then she must gybe (rule 17).

When the leeward boat sails above her proper course, without the right to do so, the windward boat must still try to keep clear (rule 11).

GYBING

A boat that is gybing does not necessarily lose her rights

Gybing in itself places no additional obligations on a boat. Only when the right-of-way boat changes course must she give room to the keep-clear boat to keep clear (rule 16.1).

gybes

I DIDN'T CHANGE COURSE AND YOU DIDN'T KEEP CLEAR

Before White gybes she is the leeward (right-of-way) boat. She may or may not have the right to sail above her proper course, depending on how the overlap was established. Without changing course she gybes on to starboard tack. At no time was she the keep-clear boat and she didn't change course, so if the booms touch, or White has to take action to prevent her boom making contact with Black's boom, then Black has broken rule 10 (the port-and-starboard rule) (rules 11 and 10).

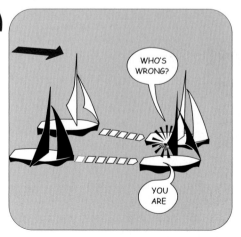

WHO'S WRONG?

YOU ARE

Simultaneous gybing

When a boat gybes, she simply changes tack when the mainsail lies on the new side. If two boats gybe at the same time without changing course, the one that gybed on to port tack is wrong, because whether or not the other boat gybes, she gybes into a keep-clear position (rule 10).

THE
FINISH

The finish ends racing; it is also
the beginning of the protest
period – when this book may
again be useful.

this boat has finished, provided she has no outstanding penalty turns relating to an incident at the finish

this boat has not finished yet because her spinnaker is not in its normal position

Finishing

A boat finishes when any part of her hull, crew or equipment in normal position, crosses the finishing line in the direction of the course from the last mark; either for the first time or, if she is taking a penalty (for hitting a finishing mark or breaking a 'when boats meet' rule, or after correcting an error made at the finishing line) (Definition of Finishing).

A boat that has finished is still racing until she has cleared the finishing line, so a boat that breaks a rule before she has cleared the finish line, but after she has finished, must take her penalty for the breach, and then finish again.

In the incident below, the port tack boat (white) would not have had to take a penalty if she had been clear of the finishing line – that is, no longer intersecting any part of it – since she would not have been racing. But here she was still racing so she must sail clear, do a Two-Turns Penalty, return to the pre-finish side of the line, and finish (rule 44.2).

To clear the finish line it is not necessary to sail right across it. The boat in the bottom picture has finished and cleared the line (Definition of Finishing) (rule 28.1).

this boat has finished but is still racing until clear of the line and is therefore in the wrong in this port and starboard incident

finishing line

finishing line

previous mark

A boat also finishes correctly when capsized and the tide carries her across the finishing line – provided all the crew are with the boat. But the crew may not swim the capsized boat to the finishing line (rule 42).

Hitting a finishing mark

If you hit a finishing mark without having cleared the finishing line, you can exonerate yourself by sailing clear of other boats and doing a penalty turn, then returning to a position wholly on the course side of the finishing line, and then finishing again. Obviously, the finishing position on the second crossing is the one that will be counted.

direction of
finishing

this boat
now wins

last mark

When a boat has crossed and cleared the finishing line and sailed clear of the marks, but then drifts or sails back and hits a finishing mark, she will not be penalized because she is no longer racing (Definition of Racing and preamble to Part 2).

The 'hook finish'

A boat sailing a hook finish doesn't actually finish according to the definition, no matter what the sailing instructions say (see next page).

Conundrum will have difficulty knowing which way to finish on this badly set short-ened-course finishing line, and the race committee will have to count as finished all the boats, whichever way they cross. Some will have finished correctly (according to the definition) and the others will have to be given redress (by way of finishing places) for the error of the race committee in setting such an impossible finishing line.

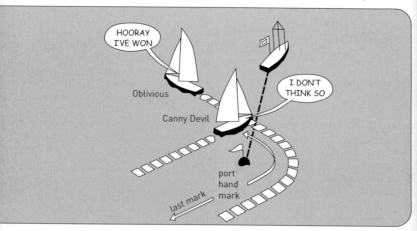

Canny Devil wins the race by being the first boat to finish in accordance with the def-inition (even if the sailing instructions said she must finish the way Oblivious did); Oblivious hasn't actually finished but she could unwind and finish correctly, or she might succeed in getting redress if she can convince a protest committee that the race committee confused her into thinking she was finishing correctly; but in giving redress, the protest committee cannot take away Canny Devil's victory.

OTHER IMPORTANT SAILING RULES, ENFORCEMENT AND PENALTIES

Competitive sailors are their own umpires. If we want our sport to stay healthy and enjoyable, every one of us has an interest in taking a penalty when we ourselves break a rule and protesting when someone else does and fails to take a penalty. Otherwise, anarchy ensues.

OTHER IMPORTANT SAILING RULES

Assisting a boat in distress

When in a position to do so, every boat must help any boat or person in danger (rule 1.1). You don't break a rule if you collide with another boat while trying to assist a boat or person in danger (rule 22). You can ask for redress to make up for any places you lose, but you can't get redress having lost places if the assistance is to your own boat or your own crew (rule 62.1(c)).

Fair sailing

The fair sailing rule (rule 2) says boats must compete in 'compliance with recognized principles of sportsmanship and fair play'. Hailing 'starboard' when you're on port, with the intention of confusing a beginner is clearly unfair (ISAF Case 47). Interfering with a rival after the start when you know you are a premature starter, or leaning out further than normal to touch a windward boat, are other examples (ISAF Cases 65 and 73). Harassing another boat to hold her back other than for the reason of improving your own overall score is obviously unfair (ISAF Case 34).

Avoiding contact and damage

Every boat must avoid contact with other boats if reasonably possible, but a right-of-way boat (or a boat entitled to room or Mark-Room) can only be penalized under this rule if there is damage or injury (rule 14).

However, if you are the right-of-way boat, you don't have to start taking avoiding action until it is clear that the other boat is not keeping clear. If a port tack boat is bearing away under your stern, there is usually nothing you can do but hope she succeeds (rule 14(a)).

If you are the right-of-way boat and you have contact which was 'reasonably possible' to avoid, and there is damage but it's not serious, you can exonerate yourself by taking a Two-Turns Penalty.

If it was 'reasonably possible' to avoid the contact, and the contact resulted in serious damage (to either boat, or even a third boat) or injury, whether the culprit was the keep-clear or the right-of-way boat you must retire (rule 44.1).

If you are the right-of-way boat and you have contact with another boat that you could have avoided, and there is no damage or injury, you need not take a penalty (rule 14(b)).

Damage is anything a prudent owner would repair. Serious damage is damage that significantly affects the performance of the boat (or its crew), makes the boat unsafe, or is expensive to repair (ISAF Case 19).

Avoiding an anchored boat, or a boat capsized or aground

Other boats must, if possible, avoid a boat that is anchored. If you're anchored you must avoid other anchored boats (rule 22).

Anchoring includes lowering any weight to the bottom, or the crew standing on the bottom holding on to the boat. Anchoring does not mean tying up to or holding on to a mooring, moored boat or jetty. Neither does it mean standing on a jetty to hold the boat. None of these actions are allowed while you're racing, unless you are bailing out, reefing your sails, or making repairs (rule 45).

Other boats must, if possible, avoid a boat that is capsized or aground. For a boat to be 'capsized', it has to have its masthead in the water, so an upright swamped dinghy on port tack with no steerage way is a sitting duck. If it's not possible to avoid a capsized boat or a boat that has run aground, because it happens suddenly in front of you, then no rule is broken, even though there might be damage (rule 22).

Propulsion

There are some exceptions, but the basic rule says 'a boat shall compete by using only the wind and water to increase, maintain or decrease her speed. Her crew may adjust the trim of sails and hull, and perform other acts of seamanship, but shall not otherwise move their bodies to propel the boat' (rule 42.1).

In general terms, this means that the crew can move their body-weight to trim the boat, but not to add energy to the boat to drive it forward. The sails can be moved to adjust for a change in wind strength or direction, but the move itself must not drive the boat forward.

There are some exceptions: you can propel your boat in any way you like if you are going to help someone in distress, or recovering a person overboard, or rendering assistance. Except on a beat, when surfing or planing conditions exist, you may pump (ie rapidly trim and release) any sail, or all sails, once, in order to *initiate* (but not to *maintain*) surfing or planing.

You can roll tack or gybe, provided that the manoeuvre doesn't mean you'd be going faster coming out of the tack or gybe than you would have been had you not tacked or gybed (rule 42.3(b)).

At many well-organized regattas, judges will be on the water and will penalize competitors they see breaking the propulsion rule. Most competitors applaud such action, which if taken early in the series, inevitably results in suppressing the problem of competitors using 'kinetics' to increase their speed.

PENALTIES AND RULE ENFORCEMENT

Disqualification

A boat that is found by a protest committee to have broken a rule or a sailing instruction is usually disqualified from the race in which the breach occurred. An exception is where a boat retires or does a Two-Turns Penalty promptly after an incident in recognition that she has broken a rule, but also protests the other boat, claiming the other boat broke a rule; if the protest committee decides that she, the protesting boat, broke a rule, she will not be disqualified because she already took a penalty (unless the penalty for the breach was a DNE – a disqualification that cannot be discarded).

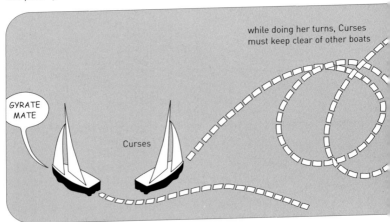

A boat can exonerate herself for breaking a 'when boats meet' rule (those in Part 2 of the rules), by taking a Two-Turns Penalty (rule 44.1). However, if she causes injury or gains a significant advantage in the race or series by her breach she must retire. A fundamental principle of sportsmanship is that when competitors break a rule they will promptly take a penalty (or retire) (Sportsmanship and the Rules).

After getting well clear of other boats as soon after the incident as possible, a boat takes a Two-Turns Penalty by promptly making two turns in the same direction, each including a tack and a gybe. When a boat takes the penalty at or near the finishing line, she must, after completing the penalty as soon as possible, sail completely to the course side of the line before finishing (rule 44.2).

The penalty turns must be done at the first reasonable opportunity. If the breach was just before the mark, this might not be until the next leg, but you must actively find a clear enough patch of water to do the turns without getting in the way of other boats; you can't sail on, waiting for a space to appear.

While getting clear, a boat intending to take a penalty does not lose her rights, but while she is doing the turns she must keep clear (rule 21.2). Except when sailing her proper course, a boat must not interfere with a boat taking a penalty (rule 23.2).

Scoring penalty

The sailing instructions can annul the Two-Turns Penalty system (in which case a boat breaking a rule must retire) or prescribe some other penalty system. The most common alternative to the Two-Turns Penalty is the 'scoring penalty' (rule 44.3).

A boat takes a scoring penalty by displaying a yellow flag at the first reasonable opportunity after the incident (rule 44.3(a)). She must then keep it displayed until finishing and informing the race committee of the identity of the other boat involved in the incident (rule 44.3(b)).

The penalty is to make the boat's score worse than her actual finishing place by 20 per cent of the number of boats entered (unless the sailing instructions give some other number). The scores of other boats are not changed; therefore two boats may receive the same score (rule 44.3(c)).

Multiple penalties

A boat that takes a penalty is not penalized further with respect to the same incident unless she failed to retire when she caused injury, serious damage or gained a significant advantage in the race or series (rule 64.1(b)).

Touching a mark

After the preparatory signal, you mustn't let any part of your boat, equipment or crew touch a starting mark or a mark that begins, bounds or ends the leg of the course on which you are sailing, or a finishing mark after finishing but before clearing the line. However, if your boat does touch a mark, you may exonerate yourself by getting well clear of other boats as soon as possible, and take a One-Turn Penalty by promptly making a turn including one tack and one gybe.

When a boat takes the penalty after touching a finishing mark, she must sail completely to the course side of the line before finishing (rule 44.2).

If a boat has gained a significant advantage in the race or series by touching the mark she must retire, even if by taking the penalty she ends up further back than she would be if she had not touched the mark (rule 44.1(b)).

If a boat breaks a 'when boats meet rule' and touches a mark, provided she does not gain a significant advantage (or cause injury or serious damage), she can exonerate herself with just one Two-Turn Penalty (rule 44.1(a)).

If a boat is wrongly compelled to touch a mark (for example if she should have been given Mark-Room and wasn't), then she need not take a penalty (rules 31 and 64.1(c)).

Even before the starting signal (but after the preparatory signal), a boat breaking a rule must do her turns as soon as possible. If the turns are not properly done and a valid protest is lodged, she will be disqualified.

When injury or serious damage is caused, the boat in the wrong must retire; if she doesn't, she may be disqualified, even though she may have done her turns properly.

It is sometimes possible for a boat to deliberately break a rule, do the Two-Turns Penalty and end up better off after the incident than she would have done by obeying the rules. A port tack boat rounding a windward mark, for example, against a strong tide in light air might lose less ground by refusing to keep clear of a starboard boat and then take the penalty turns after rounding the mark than by tacking to keep clear of the starboard boat and failing to lay the mark, or ducking behind and losing a lot of ground. The port tack boat can be disqualified after a protest even though she might have done her turns immediately after the incident (rule 44.1(b)).

Protest by one competitor against another

If you make contact with another boat and you don't think you have broken a rule, and the other boat doesn't take a penalty, you don't have to protest. Even if you hail 'protest', you don't have to go through with it. Even if it is lodged in writing, a protestor may ask for it to be withdrawn, and this will usually be allowed.

When a 'third boat' that witnesses, but is not involved in, an incident wants to protest, she must hail 'protest', or if the protested boat is too far away, inform her as soon as possible. If the third boat's protest is valid, it must be heard by the protest committee. Even if the protest was against the wrong boat, or quoted the wrong rule, the boat that broke a rule will be penalized.

When you are involved in an incident in which another boat has broken a rule, or when you are not involved but see what you think is a boat breaking a rule, and not taking a penalty, you are entitled to protest (rule 60.1(a)). A protest is decided ashore by a protest committee, which is usually a committee appointed by the race committee. It acts rather like a court of law, first hearing the evidence and then giving its verdict as to which, if any, boat (or boats) has broken a rule. Those it decides have broken a rule are disqualified.

A helmsman who decides to protest must hail 'protest' (and, if the boat's hull length is six metres or more, display a red protest flag) (rule 61.1(a)).

If you see a boat breaking a rule, but you are not involved in the incident, and you want to protest, you must hail 'protest'. If you hear that one of the boats involved is going to protest, especially if you hear him shouting 'protest', remember he might not actually lodge the protest, and if you haven't hailed, then your protest would be ruled as invalid.

On coming ashore, the boat protesting must put in a written protest to the race committee (rule 61.2). The protest must be delivered within two hours of the time the last boat finishes (unless the sailing instructions specify some different time or the protest committee has reason to extend the time), but when there is a good reason to do so, the protest committee must extend the time limit (rule 61.3).

The protestee (the representative of the protested boat) is entitled to a copy of the protest, or if that's not possible, then time to study the original. The protestee must make a reasonable attempt to find out when the protest is to be heard, and make himself available for the hearing.

Protest by a race committee or protest committee

Having seen what it thinks is a boat breaking a rule and not taking a penalty, the race committee (or the protest committee, if there is one) may protest. It obviously doesn't have to display a flag, and it doesn't have to inform the boat until after the race – too late for the boat to take a penalty (rule 61.1(b)). For what incidents should the race committee (or protest committee) protest? In my opinion, only when it sees the sort of breaches that have the effect of gaining on the rest of the fleet (like breaking the propulsion rule or hitting a mark) rather than just the other boat involved, or where there is a gross breach, damage or injury.

If the race committee believes you haven't started or finished, it can score you as DNS or DNF without a hearing. If you think the committee has made a mistake, it's best just to ask first. If the race committee doesn't fix the error (or satisfy you that it was correct) then you can ask for redress, and get a formal hearing. You should make your request in writing as soon as you can.

Disqualification without a hearing

Unless the sailing instructions have extended the power of the race committee or the protest committee to disqualify a boat without a hearing (which is often the case in major championships for breaches of rule 42 (Propulsion)), the only breaches for which a race committee may penalize a boat without a hearing are failing to start or finish correctly. (They are scored 'DNS' for 'did not start', 'OCS' for 'on the course side' of the starting line at the start, and 'DNF' for 'did not finish'.) A competitor who doesn't agree can ask for redress, but it's best to ask the race officer first (rule 60.1(b)).

Requesting redress

When a competitor believes his finishing position has been prejudiced by an improper act or omission of the race committee (or the protest committee or the organizing authority), he may make a 'request for redress' (rules 60.1(b) and 62.1(a)).

The request must be in writing and be received within the time limit for protests or within two hours of the incident (which, if it's something to do with scoring, might be after the race when the results get posted) (rule 62.2).

The protest committee must proceed with a hearing, but before even considering what redress is appropriate, it must be satisfied that the boat's finishing position in the race (or series) has been made significantly worse, and that this was through no fault of the boat. It must also be satisfied that it was due to an improper act or omission of the race committee, the protest committee or the organising authority (or one of the other reasons that allows redress to be given) (rule 62.1). If these criteria are met, it must give redress, but giving redress means making as fair an arrangement as possible for all boats affected, not just the one asking for redress. Sometimes this means letting the results stand. Often it means adjusting the points for the boat asking for redress. Very rarely is abandoning the race the best solution (rule 64.2).

Redress can also be given when a boat gives assistance to someone in distress while racing, is physically damaged by a boat breaking a 'when boats meet' rule, or is disadvantaged by a boat that is found to have broken the fair sailing rule or found guilty of 'gross misconduct' (rules 62.1 and 69.1).

Composition of a protest committee

At a local or club event, the protest committee is appointed by the race committee. No one may be on a protest committee who might benefit from that committee's decision. Interpreted strictly, this would bar competitors from protest committees, but in practice competitors can be included provided both protestor and protestee agree. So at the start of the hearing, the protestor and protestee should be asked whether they object to any member of the protest committee, those members who competed in the race or the series being pointed out. If there are no objections, then an appeal solely on the grounds that a member of the protest committee was an 'interested party' would not succeed (rule 63.4).

At major events, the organizing authority appoints a protest committee that is independent of the race committee; its decisions are usually open to appeal (even by the race committee if it doesn't agree with a decision to which it was a party) (rule 70.1).

The right to appeal

The decision of a protest committee or jury can usually be referred to the national authority in whose jurisdiction the event was held. The national authority's decision is final. The International Sailing Federation does not decide appeals. However, an appeal to the national authority can be considered only on a question of rule interpretation or procedures, not on a question of fact. The final arbiter of fact is the protest committee (rule 70.1).

For some major events like World Championships an International Jury is appointed; then there is no right of appeal. The waiving of the right to appeal is also common in two-day team racing events where teams must be eliminated from early rounds before there can be a final. An appeal of a decision in all but the final round would dislocate the whole event. Under these circumstances, the organizers can deny the right of appeal. In some countries, permission from the national authority is required, which is given when the NA approves the membership of the jury.

There is no right of appeal against a decision by an International Jury acting in accordance with Appendix N.

Counter-protest

It often happens that both boats involved in an incident lodge a protest, or one of the two involved protests and a boat not involved also protests. The validity of each protest is considered separately, and if both or all protests are valid, they are heard simultaneously if they are about the same incident, or even two closely related incidents. If one protest is found not to be valid (perhaps there was no hail) then of course it makes little difference because the other protest will be heard (ISAF Case 49).

The protest hearing

The procedure for hearing a protest is well explained in Appendix M of the rules. It is important that this is followed carefully, as major errors of procedure can result in decisions being changed on appeal. If any of the 'parties' (protestor or protestee) feel that procedural errors are being made, the issue should be raised at the time. Failure to complain at the time, or as soon as the wrong procedure became known, would mean that an appeal based on the procedural errors would be dismissed.

The protestee and the protestor have the right to be present at the hearing and throughout the taking of evidence (rule 63.3(a)). When either the protestee or protestor has made a reasonable attempt to be present he should be allowed to be present. So if a committee has several protests to hear, it should hear those where both parties are present first. But if an interested party fails to make an effort to attend the hearing, the protest committee may deal with the case in his absence (rule 63.3(b)).

The protestor and protestee may call as many witnesses as they choose, and every witness may be questioned by the committee and the other party. The protest committee will deliberate in private, and then recall the parties to announce its decision. This is in the form of 'facts found' (what it thinks happened), the 'decision' (whether a boat is to be penalized, and if so which one(s)), the 'grounds for the decision' and the rule numbers that apply. Any party can get a written copy if they ask for it in writing within seven days (rule 65.2).

THE RACING RULES OF SAILING

2009–2012 rules

CONTENTS

INTRODUCTION

The Racing Rules of Sailing includes two main sections. The first, Parts 1–7, contains rules that affect all competitors. The second, Appendices A–P, provides details of rules, rules that apply to particular kinds of racing, and rules that affect only a small number of competitors or officials.

Revision   The racing rules are revised and published every four years by the International Sailing Federation (ISAF), the international authority for the sport. This edition becomes effective on 1 January 2009 except that for an event beginning in 2008 the date may be postponed by the notice of race and sailing instructions. Marginal markings indicate important changes to Parts 1–7 and the Definitions of the 2005–2008 edition. No changes are contemplated before 2013, but any changes determined to be urgent before then will be announced through national authorities and posted on the ISAF website (www.sailing.org).

ISAF Codes   The ISAF Eligibility, Advertising, Anti-Doping and Sailor Classification Codes (Regulations 19, 20, 21 and 22) are referred to in the definition *Rule* but are not included in this book because they can be changed at any time. The most recent versions of the codes are available on the ISAF website; new versions will be announced through national authorities.

Cases and Calls   The ISAF publishes interpretations of the racing rules in *The Case Book for 2009–2012* and recognizes them as authoritative interpretations and explanations of the rules. It also publishes *The Call Book for Match Racing for 2009–2012* and *The Call Book for Team Racing for 2009–2012*, and it recognizes them as authoritative only for umpired match or team racing. These publications are available on the ISAF website.

Terminology   A term used in the sense stated in the Definitions is printed in italics or, in preambles, in bold italics (for example, *racing* and *racing*). 'Racing rule' means a rule in *The Racing Rules of Sailing*. 'Boat' means a sailboat and the crew on board. 'Race committee' includes any person or committee performing a race committee function. A 'change' to a *rule* includes an addition to it or deletion of all or part of it. 'National authority' means an ISAF member national authority. Other words and terms are used in the sense ordinarily understood in nautical or general use.

Appendices When the rules of an appendix apply, they take precedence over any conflicting rules in Parts 1–7 and the Definitions. Each appendix is identified by a letter. A reference to a rule in an appendix will contain the letter and the rule number (for example, 'rule A1'). There is no Appendix I or O.

Changes to the Rules The prescriptions of a national authority, class rules or the sailing instructions may change a racing rule only as permitted in rule 86.

Changes to National Authority Prescriptions A national authority may restrict changes to its prescriptions as provided in rule 88.2.

BASIC PRINCIPLE

SPORTSMANSHIP AND THE RULES
Competitors in the sport of sailing are governed by a body of *rules* that they are expected to follow and enforce. A fundamental principle of sportsmanship is that when competitors break a *rule* they will promptly take a penalty, which may be to retire.

PART 1 – FUNDAMENTAL RULES

1   **SAFETY**

1.1   **Helping Those in Danger**
A boat or competitor shall give all possible help to any person or vessel in danger.

1.2   **Life-Saving Equipment and Personal Flotation Devices**
A boat shall carry adequate life-saving equipment for all persons on board, including one item ready for immediate use, unless her class rules make some other provision. Each competitor is individually responsible for wearing a personal flotation device adequate for the conditions.

2 **FAIR SAILING**

A boat and her owner shall compete in compliance with recognized principles of sportsmanship and fair play. A boat may be penalized under this rule only if it is clearly established that these principles have been violated. A disqualification under this rule shall not be excluded from the boat's series score.

3 **ACCEPTANCE OF THE RULES**

By participating in a race conducted under these racing rules, each competitor and boat owner agrees
(a) to be governed by the *rules*;
(b) to accept the penalties imposed and other action taken under the *rules*, subject to the appeal and review procedures provided in them, as the final determination of any matter arising under the *rules*; and
(c) with respect to any such determination, not to resort to any court of law or tribunal.

4 **DECISION TO RACE**

The responsibility for a boat's decision to participate in a race or to continue *racing* is hers alone.

5 **ANTI-DOPING**

A competitor shall comply with the World Anti-Doping Code, the rules of the World Anti-Doping Agency, and ISAF Regulation 21, Anti-Doping Code. An alleged or actual breach of this rule shall be dealt with under Regulation 21. It shall not be grounds for a *protest* and rule 63.1 does not apply.

PART 2 – WHEN BOATS MEET

The rules of Part 2 apply between boats that are sailing in or near the racing area and intend to **race**, *are* **racing**, *or have been* **racing**. *However, a boat not* **racing** *shall not be penalized for breaking one of these rules, except rule 23.1. When a boat sailing under these rules meets a vessel that is not, she shall comply with the* International Regulations for Preventing Collisions at Sea (IRPCAS) *or government right-of-way rules. If the sailing instructions so state, the rules of Part 2 are replaced by the right-of-way rules of the IRPCAS or by government right-of-way rules.*

Section A – Right of Way

A boat has right of way when another boat is required to **keep clear** *of her. However, some rules in Sections B, C and D limit the actions of a right-of-way boat.*

10   ON OPPOSITE TACKS

When boats are on opposite *tacks*, a *port-tack* boat shall *keep clear* of a *starboard-tack* boat.

11   ON THE SAME TACK, OVERLAPPED

When boats are on the same *tack* and *overlapped*, a *windward* boat shall *keep clear* of a *leeward* boat.

12   ON THE SAME TACK, NOT OVERLAPPED

When boats are on the same *tack* and not *overlapped*, a boat *clear astern* shall *keep clear* of a boat *clear ahead*.

13   WHILE TACKING

After a boat passes head to wind, she shall *keep clear* of other boats until she is on a close-hauled course. During that time rules 10, 11 and 12 do not apply. If two boats are subject to this rule at the same time, the one on the other's port side or the one astern shall *keep clear*.

Section B – General Limitations

14   AVOIDING CONTACT

A boat shall avoid contact with another boat if reasonably possible. However, a right-of-way boat or one entitled to *room* or *Mark-Room*

(a)   need not act to avoid contact until it is clear that the other boat is not *keeping clear* or giving *room* or *Mark-Room*, and

(b)   shall not be penalized under this rule unless there is contact that causes damage or injury.

15   ACQUIRING RIGHT OF WAY

When a boat acquires right of way, she shall initially give the other boat *room* to *keep clear*, unless she acquires right of way because of the other boat's actions.

16   CHANGING COURSE

16.1 When a right-of-way boat changes course, she shall give the other boat *room* to *keep clear*.

16.2 In addition, when after the starting signal a *port-tack* boat is *keeping clear* by sailing to pass astern of a *starboard-tack* boat, the *starboard-tack* boat shall not change course if as a result the *port-tack* boat would immediately need to change course to continue *keeping clear*.

17 ON THE SAME TACK; PROPER COURSE

If a boat *clear astern* becomes *overlapped* within two of her hull lengths to *leeward* of a boat on the same *tack*, she shall not sail above her *proper course* while they remain on the same *tack* and *overlapped* within that distance, unless in doing so she promptly sails astern of the other boat. This rule does not apply if the *overlap* begins while the *windward* boat is required by rule 13 to *keep clear*.

Section C – At Marks and Obstructions

Section C rules do not apply at a starting **mark** *surrounded by navigable water or at its anchor line from the time boats are approaching them to* **start** *until they have passed them. When rule 20 applies, rules 18 and 19 do not.*

18 MARK-ROOM

18.1 When Rule 18 Applies

Rule 18 applies between boats when they are required to leave a *mark* on the same side and at least one of them is in the *zone*. However, it does not apply

(a) between boats on opposite *tacks* on a beat to windward,

(b) between boats on opposite *tacks* when the *proper course* at the *mark* for one but not both of them is to tack,

(c) between a boat approaching a *mark* and one leaving it, or

(d) if the *mark* is a continuing *obstruction*, in which case rule 19 applies.

18.2 Giving Mark-Room

(a) When boats are *overlapped* the outside boat shall give the inside boat *Mark-Room*, unless rule 18.2(b) applies.

(b) If boats are *overlapped* when the first of them reaches the *zone*, the outside boat at that moment shall thereafter give the inside boat *Mark-Room*. If a boat is *clear ahead* when she reaches the *zone*, the boat *clear astern* at that moment shall thereafter give her *Mark-Room*.

(c) When a boat is required to give *Mark-Room* by rule 18.2(b), she shall continue to do so even if later an *overlap* is broken or a new *overlap* begins. However, if either boat passes head to wind or if the boat entitled to *Mark-Room* leaves the *zone*, rule 18.2(b) ceases to apply.

(d) If there is reasonable doubt that a boat obtained or broke an *overlap* in time, it shall be presumed that she did not.

(e) If a boat obtained an inside *overlap* from *clear astern* and, from the time the *overlap* began, the outside boat has been unable to give *Mark-Room*, she is not required to give it.

18.3 Tacking When Approaching a Mark

If two boats were approaching a *mark* on opposite *tacks* and one of them changes *tack*, and as a result is subject to rule 13 in the *zone* when the other is *fetching* the *mark*, rule 18.2 does not thereafter apply. The boat that changed *tack*

(a) shall not cause the other boat to sail above close-hauled to avoid her or prevent the other boat from passing the *mark* on the required side, and

(b) shall give *Mark-Room* if the other boat becomes *overlapped* inside her.

18.4 Gybing

When an inside *overlapped* right-of-way boat must gybe at a *mark* to sail her *proper course*, until she gybes she shall sail no farther from the *mark* than needed to sail that course. Rule 18.4 does not apply at a gate *mark*.

18.5 Exoneration

When a boat is taking *Mark-Room* to which she is entitled, she shall be exonerated

(a) if, as a result of the other boat failing to give her *Mark-Room*, she breaks a rule of Section A, or

(b) if, by rounding the *mark* on her *proper course*, she breaks a rule of Section A or rule 15 or 16.

19 ROOM TO PASS AN OBSTRUCTION

19.1 When Rule 19 Applies

Rule 19 applies between boats at an *obstruction* except when it is also a *mark* the boats are required to leave on the same side.

However, at a continuing *obstruction*, rule 19 always applies and rule 18 does not.

19.2 Giving Room at an Obstruction

(a) A right-of-way boat may choose to pass an *obstruction* on either side.

(b) When boats are *overlapped*, the outside boat shall give the inside boat *room* between her and the *obstruction*, unless she has been unable to do so from the time the *overlap* began.

(c) While boats are passing a continuing *obstruction*, if a boat that was *clear astern* and required to *keep clear* becomes *overlapped* between the other boat and the *obstruction* and, at the moment the *overlap* begins, there is not *room* for her to pass between them, she is not entitled to *room* under rule 19.2(b). While the boats remain *overlapped*, she shall *keep clear* and rules 10 and 11 do not apply.

20 ROOM TO TACK AT AN OBSTRUCTION

20.1 Hailing and Responding

When approaching an *obstruction*, a boat sailing close-hauled or above may hail for *room* to tack and avoid another boat on the same *tack*. After a boat hails,

(a) she shall give the hailed boat time to respond;

(b) the hailed boat shall respond either by tacking as soon as possible, or by immediately replying 'You tack' and then giving the hailing boat *room* to tack and avoid her; and

(c) when the hailed boat responds, the hailing boat shall tack as soon as possible.

20.2 Exoneration

When a boat is taking *room* to which she is entitled under rule 20.1(b), she shall be exonerated if she breaks a rule of Section A or rule 15 or 16.

20.3 When Not to Hail

A boat shall not hail unless safety requires her to make a substantial course change to avoid the *obstruction*. Also, she shall not hail if the *obstruction* is a *mark* that the hailed boat is *fetching*.

Section D – Other Rules

When rule 21 or 22 applies between two boats, Section A rules do not.

21   STARTING ERRORS; TAKING PENALTIES; MOVING ASTERN

21.1   A boat sailing towards the pre-start side of the starting line or one of its extensions after her starting signal to *start* or to comply with rule 30.1 shall *keep clear* of a boat not doing so until she is completely on the pre-start side.

21.2   A boat taking a penalty shall *keep clear* of one that is not.

21.3   A boat moving astern by backing a sail shall *keep clear* of one that is not.

22   CAPSIZED, ANCHORED OR AGROUND; RESCUING
If possible, a boat shall avoid a boat that is capsized or has not regained control after capsizing, is anchored or aground, or is trying to help a person or vessel in danger. A boat is capsized when her masthead is in the water.

23   INTERFERING WITH ANOTHER BOAT

23.1   If reasonably possible, a boat not *racing* shall not interfere with a boat that is *racing*.

23.2   Except when sailing her *proper course*, a boat shall not interfere with a boat taking a penalty or sailing on another leg.

PART 3 – CONDUCT OF A RACE

25   NOTICE OF RACE, SAILING INSTRUCTIONS AND SIGNALS
The notice of race and sailing instructions shall be made available to each boat before a race begins. The meanings of the visual and sound signals stated in Race Signals shall not be changed except under rule 86.1(b). The meanings of any other signals that may be used shall be stated in the sailing instructions.

26 STARTING RACES

Races shall be started by using the following signals. Times shall be taken from the visual signals; the absence of a sound signal shall be disregarded.

Signal	Flag and sound	Minutes before starting signal
Warning	Class flag; 1 sound	5*
Preparatory	P, I, Z, Z with I, or black flag; 1 sound	4
One-minute	Preparatory flag removed; 1 long sound	1
Starting	Class flag removed; 1 sound	0

*or as stated in the sailing instructions

The warning signal for each succeeding class shall be made with or after the starting signal of the preceding class.

27 OTHER RACE COMMITTEE ACTIONS BEFORE THE STARTING SIGNAL

27.1 No later than the warning signal, the race committee shall signal or otherwise designate the course to be sailed if the sailing instructions have not stated the course, and it may replace one course signal with another and signal that wearing personal flotation devices is required (display flag Y with one sound).

27.2 No later than the preparatory signal, the race commit-tee may move a starting *mark*.

27.3 Before the starting signal, the race committee may for any reason *postpone* (display flag AP, AP over H, or AP over A, with two sounds) or *abandon* the race (display flag N over H, or N over A, with three sounds).

28 SAILING THE COURSE

28.1 A boat shall *start*, leave each *mark* on the required side in the correct order, and *finish*, so that a string representing her track after *starting* and until *finishing* would when drawn taut

(a) pass each *mark* on the required side,

   (b)   touch each rounding *mark*, and

   (c)   pass between the *marks* of a gate from the direction of the previous *mark*.

She may correct any errors to comply with this rule. After *finishing* she need not cross the finishing line completely.

28.2   A boat may leave on either side a *mark* that does not begin, bound or end the leg she is on. However, she shall leave a starting *mark* on the required side when she is approaching the starting line from its pre-start side to *start*.

29   RECALLS

29.1   Individual Recall

When at a boat's starting signal any part of her hull, crew or equipment is on the course side of the starting line or she must comply with rule 30.1, the race committee shall promptly display flag X with one sound. The flag shall be displayed until all such boats are completely on the pre-start side of the starting line or one of its extensions and have complied with rule 30.1 if it applies, but no later than four minutes after the starting signal or one minute before any later starting signal, whichever is earlier. If rule 30.3 applies this rule does not.

29.2   General Recall

When at the starting signal the race committee is unable to identify boats that are on the course side of the starting line or to which rule 30 applies, or there has been an error in the starting procedure, the race committee may signal a general recall (display the First Substitute with two sounds). The warning signal for a new start for the recalled class shall be made one minute after the First Substitute is removed (one sound), and the starts for any succeeding classes shall follow the new start.

30   STARTING PENALTIES

30.1   I Flag Rule

If flag I has been displayed, and any part of a boat's hull, crew or equipment is on the course side of the starting line or one of its extensions during the last minute before her starting signal, she shall thereafter sail from the course side across an extension to the pre-start side before *starting*.

30.2 Z Flag Rule

If flag Z has been displayed, no part of a boat's hull, crew or equipment shall be in the triangle formed by the ends of the starting line and the first *mark* during the last minute before her starting signal. If a boat breaks this rule and is identified, she shall receive, without a hearing, a 20% Scoring Penalty calculated as stated in rule 44.3(c). She shall be penalized even if the race is restarted or resailed, but not if it is *postponed* or *abandoned* before the starting signal. If she is similarly identified during a subsequent attempt to start the same race, she shall receive an additional 20% Scoring Penalty.

30.3 Black Flag Rule

If a black flag has been displayed, no part of a boat's hull, crew or equipment shall be in the triangle formed by the ends of the starting line and the first *mark* during the last minute before her starting signal. If a boat breaks this rule and is identified, she shall be disqualified without a hearing, even if the race is restarted or resailed, but not if it is *postponed* or *abandoned* before the starting signal. If a general recall is signalled or the race is *abandoned* after the starting signal, the race committee shall display her sail number before the next warning signal for that race, and if the race is restarted or resailed she shall not sail in it. If she does so, her disqualification shall not be excluded in calculating her series score.

31 TOUCHING A MARK

While *racing*, a boat shall not touch a starting *mark* before *starting*, a *mark* that begins, bounds or ends the leg of the course on which she is sailing, or a finishing *mark* after *finishing*.

32 SHORTENING OR ABANDONING AFTER THE START

32.1

After the starting signal, the race committee may shorten the course (display flag S with two sounds) or *abandon* the race (display flag N, N over H, or N over A, with three sounds), as appropriate,

(a)   because of an error in the starting procedure,

(b)   because of foul weather,

(c)   because of insufficient wind making it unlikely that any boat will *finish* within the time limit,

(d)   because a *mark* is missing or out of position, or

(e)   for any other reason directly affecting the safety or fairness of the competition, or may shorten the course so that other scheduled races can be sailed. However, after one boat has sailed the course and *finished* within the time limit, if any, the race committee shall not *abandon* the race without considering the consequences for all boats in the race or series.

32.2 If the race committee signals a shortened course (displays flag S with two sounds), the finishing line shall be,

(a) at a rounding *mark*, between the *mark* and a staff displaying flag S;
(b) at a line boats are required to cross at the end of each lap, that line;
(c) at a gate, between the gate *marks*.

The shortened course shall be signalled before the first boat crosses the finishing line.

33   CHANGING THE NEXT LEG OF THE COURSE

The race committee may change a leg of the course that begins at a rounding *mark* or at a gate by changing the position of the next *mark* (or the finishing line) and signalling all boats before they begin the leg. The next *mark* need not be in position at that time.

(a) If the direction of the leg will be changed, the signal shall be the display of flag C with repetitive sounds and either
(1) the new compass bearing or
(2) a green triangular flag or board for a change to starboard or a red rectangular flag or board for a change to port.
(b) If the length of the leg will be changed, the signal shall be the display of flag C with repetitive sounds and a '–' if the length will be decreased or a '+' if it will be increased.
(c) Subsequent legs may be changed without further signalling to maintain the course shape.

34   MARK MISSING

If a *mark* is missing or out of position, the race committee shall, if possible,
(a) replace it in its correct position or substitute a new one of similar appearance, or
(b) substitute an object displaying flag M and make repetitive sound signals.

35   TIME LIMIT AND SCORES
If one boat sails the course as required by rule 28.1 and *finishes* within the time limit, if any, all boats that *finish* shall be scored according to their finishing places unless the race is *abandoned*. If no boat *finishes* within the time limit, the race committee shall *abandon* the race.

36   RACES RESTARTED OR RESAILED
If a race is restarted or resailed, a breach of a *rule*, other than rule 30.3, in the original race shall not prohibit a boat from competing or, except under rule 30.2, 30.3 or 69, cause her to be penalized.

PART 4 – OTHER REQUIREMENTS WHEN RACING

Part 4 rules apply only to boats **racing**.

40   PERSONAL FLOTATION DEVICES
When flag Y is displayed with one sound before or with the warning signal, competitors shall wear personal flotation devices, except briefly while changing or adjusting clothing or personal equipment. Wet suits and dry suits are not personal flotation devices.

41   OUTSIDE HELP
A boat shall not receive help from any outside source, except

(a)   help for an ill or injured crew member;
(b)   after a collision, help from the crew of the other boat to get clear;
(c)   help in the form of information freely available to all boats;
(d)   unsolicited information from a disinterested source, which may be another boat in the same race.

42   PROPULSION

42.1   Basic Rule
Except when permitted in rule 42.3 or 45, a boat shall compete

by using only the wind and water to increase, maintain or decrease her speed. Her crew may adjust the trim of sails and hull, and perform other acts of seamanship, but shall not otherwise move their bodies to propel the boat.

42.2   Prohibited Actions

Without limiting the application of rule 42.1, these actions are prohibited:

(a)   pumping: repeated fanning of any sail either by pulling in and releasing the sail or by vertical or athwartship body movement;

(b)   rocking: repeated rolling of the boat, induced by
   (1)   body movement,
   (2)   repeated adjustment of the sails or centre-board, or
   (3)   steering;

(c)   ooching: sudden forward body movement, stopped abruptly;

(d)   sculling: repeated movement of the helm that is either forceful or that propels the boat forward or prevents her from moving astern;

(e)   repeated tacks or gybes unrelated to changes in the wind or to tactical considerations.

42.3   Exceptions

(a)   A boat may be rolled to facilitate steering.

(b)   A boat's crew may move their bodies to exaggerate the rolling that facilitates steering the boat through a tack or a gybe, provided that, just after the tack or gybe is completed, the boat's speed is not greater than it would have been in the absence of the tack or gybe.

(c)   Except on a beat to windward, when surfing (rapidly accelerating down the leeward side of a wave) or planing is possible, the boat's crew may pull the sheet and the guy controlling any sail in order to initiate surfing or planing, but only once for each wave or gust of wind.

(d)   When a boat is above a close-hauled course and either stationary or moving slowly, she may scull to turn to a close-hauled course.

(e)   A boat may reduce speed by repeatedly moving her helm.

(f)   Any means of propulsion may be used to help a person or another vessel in danger.

(g)   To get clear after grounding or colliding with another boat or object, a boat may use force applied by the crew of either boat and any equipment other than a propulsion engine.

(h) Sailing instructions may, in stated circumstances, permit propulsion using an engine or any other method, provided the boat does not gain a significant advantage in the race.

Note: Interpretations of rule 42 are available at the ISAF website (www.sailing.org) or by mail upon request.

43 COMPETITOR CLOTHING AND EQUIPMENT

43.1 (a) Competitors shall not wear or carry clothing or equipment for the purpose of increasing their weight.

(b) Furthermore, a competitor's clothing and equipment shall not weigh more than 8 kilograms, excluding a hiking or trapeze harness and clothing (including footwear) worn only below the knee. Class rules or sailing instructions may specify a lower weight or a higher weight up to 10 kilograms. Class rules may include footwear and other clothing worn below the knee within that weight. A hiking or trapeze harness shall have positive buoyancy and shall not weigh more than 2 kilograms, except that class rules may specify a higher weight up to 4 kilograms. Weights shall be determined as required by Appendix H.

(c) When an equipment inspector or a measurer in charge of weighing clothing and equipment believes a competitor may have broken rule 43.1(a) or 43.1(b) he shall report the matter in writing to the race committee.

43.2 Rule 43.1(b) does not apply to boats required to be equipped with lifelines.

44 PENALTIES AT THE TIME OF AN INCIDENT

44.1 Taking a Penalty

A boat may take a Two-Turns Penalty when she may have broken a rule of Part 2 while *racing* or a One-Turn Penalty when she may have broken rule 31. Sailing instructions may specify the use of the Scoring Penalty or some other penalty. However,

(a) when a boat may have broken a rule of Part 2 and rule 31 in the same incident she need not take the penalty for breaking rule 31;

(b)   if the boat caused injury or serious damage or gained a significant advantage in the race or series by her breach her penalty shall be to retire.

44.2   One-Turn and Two-Turns Penalties

After getting well clear of other boats as soon after the incident as possible, a boat takes a One-Turn or Two-Turns Penalty by promptly making the required number of turns in the same direction, each turn including one tack and one gybe. When a boat takes the penalty at or near the finishing line, she shall sail completely to the course side of the line before *finishing*.

44.3   Scoring Penalty

(a)   A boat takes a Scoring Penalty by displaying a yellow flag at the first reasonable opportunity after the incident.

(b)   When a boat has taken a Scoring Penalty, she shall keep the yellow flag displayed until *finishing* and call the race committee's attention to it at the finishing line. At that time she shall also inform the race committee of the identity of the other boat involved in the incident. If this is impracticable, she shall do so at the first reasonable opportunity and within the time limit for *protests*.

(c)   The race score for a boat that takes a Scoring Penalty shall be the score she would have received without that penalty, made worse by the number of places stated in the sailing instructions. However, she shall not be scored worse than Did Not Finish. When the sailing instructions do not state the number of places, the number shall be the whole number (rounding 0.5 upward) nearest to 20% of the number of boats entered. The scores of other boats shall not be changed; therefore, two boats may receive the same score.

45   HAULING OUT; MAKING FAST; ANCHORING

A boat shall be afloat and off moorings at her preparatory signal. Thereafter, she shall not be hauled out or made fast except to bail out, reef sails or make repairs. She may anchor or the crew may stand on the bottom. She shall recover the anchor before continuing in the race unless she is unable to do so.

46   PERSON IN CHARGE

A boat shall have on board a person in charge designated by the member or organization that entered the boat. See rule 75.

47   **LIMITATIONS ON EQUIPMENT AND CREW**

47.1   A boat shall use only the equipment on board at her preparatory signal.

47.2   No person on board shall intentionally leave, except when ill or injured, or to help a person or vessel in danger, or to swim. A person leaving the boat by accident or to swim shall be back on board before the boat continues in the race.

48   **FOG SIGNALS AND LIGHTS**
      When safety requires, a boat shall sound fog signals and show lights as required by the *International Regulations for Preventing Collisions at Sea* or applicable government rules.

49   **CREW POSITION**

49.1   Competitors shall use no device designed to position their bodies outboard, other than hiking straps and stiffeners worn under the thighs.

49.2   When lifelines are required by the class rules or the sailing instructions they shall be taut, and competitors shall not position any part of their torsos outside them, except briefly to perform a necessary task. On boats equipped with upper and lower lifelines of wire, a competitor sitting on the deck facing outboard with his waist inside the lower lifeline may have the upper part of his body outside the upper lifeline.

50   **SETTING AND SHEETING SAILS**

50.1   **Changing Sails**
      When headsails or spinnakers are being changed, a replacing sail may be fully set and trimmed before the replaced sail is lowered. However, only one mainsail and, except when changing, only one spinnaker shall be carried set at a time.

50.2   **Spinnaker Poles; Whisker Poles**
      Only one spinnaker pole or whisker pole shall be used at a time except when gybing. When in use, it shall be attached to the foremost mast.

50.3   **Use of Outriggers**

(a) No sail shall be sheeted over or through an outrigger, except as permitted in rule 50.3(b) or 50.3(c). An outrigger is any fitting or other device so placed that it could exert outward pressure on a sheet or sail at a point from which, with the boat upright, a vertical line would fall outside the hull or deck planking. For the purpose of this rule, bulwarks, rails and rubbing strakes are not part of the hull or deck planking and the following are not outriggers: a bowsprit used to secure the tack of a working sail, a bumkin used to sheet the boom of a working sail, or a boom of a boomed headsail that requires no adjustment when tacking.

(b) Any sail may be sheeted to or led above a boom that is regularly used for a working sail and is permanently attached to the mast from which the head of the working sail is set.

(c) A headsail may be sheeted or attached at its clew to a spinnaker pole or whisker pole, provided that a spinnaker is not set.

50.4 **Headsails**

The difference between a headsail and a spinnaker is that the mid-girth of a headsail, measured from the mid-points of its luff and leech, does not exceed 50% of the length of its foot, and no other intermediate girth exceeds a percentage similarly proportional to its distance from the head of the sail. A sail tacked down behind the foremost mast is not a headsail.

51 **MOVABLE BALLAST**

All movable ballast, including sails that are not set, shall be properly stowed. Water, dead weight or ballast shall not be moved for the purpose of changing trim or stability. Floorboards, bulkheads, doors, stairs and water tanks shall be left in place and all cabin fixtures kept on board. However, bilge water may be bailed out.

52 **MANUAL POWER**

A boat's standing rigging, running rigging, spars and movable hull appendages shall be adjusted and operated only by manual power.

53 **SKIN FRICTION**

A boat shall not eject or release a substance, such as a polymer, or have specially textured surfaces that could improve the character of the flow of water inside the boundary layer.

54   FORESTAYS AND HEADSAIL TACKS

Forestays and headsail tacks, except those of spinnaker staysails when the boat is not close-hauled, shall be attached approximately on a boat's centreline.

PART 5 – PROTESTS, REDRESS, HEARINGS, MISCONDUCT AND APPEALS

Section A – Protests; Redress; Rule 69 Action

60   RIGHT TO PROTEST; RIGHT TO REQUEST REDRESS OR RULE 69 ACTION

60.1   A boat may

(a)   protest another boat, but not for an alleged breach of a rule of Part 2 unless she was involved in or saw the incident; or

(b)   request redress.

60.2   A race committee may

(a)   protest a boat, but not as a result of information arising from a request for redress or an invalid *protest*, or from a report from an *interested party* other than the representative of the boat herself;

(b)   request redress for a boat; or

(c)   report to the protest committee requesting action under rule 69.1(a).

However, when the race committee receives a report required by rule 43.1(c) or 78.3, it shall protest the boat.

60.3   A protest committee may

(a)   protest a boat, but not as a result of information arising from a request for redress or an invalid *protest*, or
from a report from an *interested party* other than the representative of the boat herself. However, it may protest a
boat

 (1)   if it learns of an incident involving her that may
have resulted in injury or serious damage, or

 (2)   if during the hearing of a valid *protest* it learns that
the boat, although not a *party* to the hearing, was
involved in the incident and may have broken a *rule*;

(b)   call a hearing to consider redress; or

(c)   act under rule 69.1(a).

61   PROTEST REQUIREMENTS

61.1   Informing the Protestee

(a)   A boat intending to protest shall inform the other boat at
the first reasonable opportunity. When her *protest* concerns an incident in the racing area that she is involved in
or sees, she shall hail 'Protest' and conspicuously display
a red flag at the first reasonable opportunity for each. She
shall display the flag until she is no longer *racing*.
However,

 (1)   if the other boat is beyond hailing distance, the
protesting boat need not hail but she shall inform
the other boat at the first reasonable opportunity;

 (2)   if the hull length of the protesting boat is less than 6
metres, she need not display a red flag;

 (3)   if the incident results in damage or injury that is
obvious to the boats involved and one of them
intends to protest, the requirements of this rule do
not apply to her, but she shall attempt to inform the
other boat within the time limit of rule 61.3.

(b)   A race committee or protest committee intending to
protest a boat shall inform her as soon as reasonably possible. However, if the *protest* arises from an incident the
committee observes in the racing area, it shall inform the
boat after the race within the time limit of rule 61.3.

(c)   If the protest committee decides to protest a boat under
rule 60.3(a)(2), it shall inform her as soon as reasonably
possible, close the current hearing, proceed as required by
rules 61.2 and 63, and hear the original and the new
protests together.

61.2 Protest Contents

A *protest* shall be in writing and identify

(a) the protestor and protestee;
(b) the incident, including where and when it occurred;
(c) any *rule* the protestor believes was broken; and
(d) the name of the protestor's representative.

However, if requirement (b) is met, requirement (a) may be met at any time before the hearing, and requirements (c) and (d) may be met before or during the hearing.

61.3 Protest Time Limit

A *protest* by a boat, or by the race committee or protest committee about an incident the committee observes in the racing area, shall be delivered to the race office within the time limit stated in the sailing instructions. If none is stated, the time limit is two hours after the last boat in the race *finishes*. Other race committee or protest committee *protests* shall be delivered to the race office no later than two hours after the committee receives the relevant information. The protest committee shall extend the time if there is good reason to do so.

62 REDRESS

62.1

A request for redress or a protest committee's decision to consider redress shall be based on a claim or possibility that a boat's score in a race or series has, through no fault of her own, been made significantly worse by

(a) an improper action or omission of the race committee, protest committee or organizing authority, but not by a protest committee decision when the boat was a *party* to the hearing;
(b) injury or physical damage because of the action of a boat that was breaking a rule of Part 2 or of a vessel not *racing* that was required to keep clear;
(c) giving help (except to herself or her crew) in compliance with rule 1.1; or
(d) a boat against which a penalty has been imposed under rule 2 or disciplinary action has been taken under rule 69.1(b).

62.2

The request shall be in writing and be delivered to the race office no later than the protest time limit or two hours after the incident, whichever is later. The protest committee shall extend the time if there is good reason to do so. No red flag is required.

Section B – Hearings and Decisions

63   HEARINGS

63.1   Requirement for a Hearing

A boat or competitor shall not be penalized without a protest hearing, except as provided in rules 30.2, 30.3, 67, 69, A5 and P2. A decision on redress shall not be made without a hearing. The protest committee shall hear all *protests* and requests for redress that have been delivered to the race office unless it allows a *protest* or request to be withdrawn.

63.2   Time and Place of the Hearing; Time for Parties to Prepare

All *parties* to the hearing shall be notified of the time and place of the hearing, the *protest* or redress information shall be made available to them, and they shall be allowed reasonable time to prepare for the hearing.

63.3   Right to Be Present

(a)   The *parties* to the hearing, or a representative of each, have the right to be present throughout the hearing of all the evidence. When a *protest* claims a breach of a rule of Part 2, 3 or 4, the representatives of boats shall have been on board at the time of the incident, unless there is good reason for the protest committee to rule otherwise. Any witness, other than a member of the protest committee, shall be excluded except when giving evidence.

(b)   If a *party* to the hearing of a *protest* or request for redress does not come to the hearing, the protest committee may nevertheless decide the *protest* or request. If the party was unavoidably absent, the committee may reopen the hearing.

63.4   Interested Party

A member of a protest committee who is an *interested party* shall not take any further part in the hearing but may appear as a witness. Protest committee members must declare any possible self-interest as soon as they are aware of it. A *party* to the hearing who believes a member of the protest committee is an *interested* party shall object as soon as possible.

63.5 Validity of the Protest or Request for Redress

At the beginning of the hearing the protest committee shall take any evidence it considers necessary to decide whether all requirements for the *protest* or request for redress have been met. If they have been met, the *protest* or request is valid and the hearing shall be continued. If not, the committee shall declare the *protest* or request invalid and close the hearing. If the *protest* has been made under rule 60.3(a)(1), the committee shall also determine whether or not injury or serious damage resulted from the incident in question. If not, the hearing shall be closed.

63.6 Taking Evidence and Finding Facts

The protest committee shall take the evidence of the *parties* to the hearing and of their witnesses and other evidence it considers necessary. A member of the protest committee who saw the incident may give evidence. A *party* to the hearing may question any person who gives evidence. The committee shall then find the facts and base its decision on them.

63.7 Conflict between the Notice of Race and the Sailing Instructions

If there is a conflict between a rule in the notice of race and one in the sailing instructions that must be resolved before the protest committee can decide a *protest* or request for redress, the committee shall apply the rule that it believes will provide the fairest result for all boats affected.

63.8 Protests between Boats in Different Races

A *protest* between boats sailing in different races conducted by different organizing authorities shall be heard by a protest committee acceptable to those authorities.

64 DECISIONS

64.1 Penalties and Exoneration

(a) When the protest committee decides that a boat that is a *party* to a protest hearing has broken a *rule*, it shall disqualify her unless some other penalty applies. A penalty shall be imposed whether or not the applicable *rule* was mentioned in the *protest*.

(b)   If a boat has taken an applicable penalty, rule 64.1(a) does not apply to her unless the penalty for a *rule* she broke is a disqualification that is not excludable from her series score.

(c)   When as a consequence of breaking a *rule* a boat has compelled another boat to break a *rule*, rule 64.1(a) does not apply to the other boat and she shall be exonerated.

(d)   If a boat has broken a *rule* when not *racing*, her penalty shall apply to the race sailed nearest in time to that of the incident.

64.2   Decisions on Redress

When the protest committee decides that a boat is entitled to redress under rule 62, it shall make as fair an arrangement as possible for all boats affected, whether or not they asked for redress. This may be to adjust the scoring (see rule A10 for some examples) or finishing times of boats, to *abandon* the race, to let the results stand or to make some other arrangement. When in doubt about the facts or probable results of any arrangement for the race or series, especially before *abandoning* the race, the protest committee shall take evidence from appropriate sources.

64.3   Decisions on Measurement Protests

(a)   When the protest committee finds that deviations in excess of tolerances specified in the class rules were caused by damage or normal wear and do not improve the performance of the boat, it shall not penalize her. However, the boat shall not *race* again until the deviations have been corrected, except when the protest committee decides there is or has been no reasonable opportunity to do so.

(b)   When the protest committee is in doubt about the meaning of a measurement rule, it shall refer its questions, together with the relevant facts, to an authority responsible for interpreting the rule. In making its decision, the committee shall be bound by the reply of the authority.

(c)   When a boat disqualified under a measurement rule states in writing that she intends to appeal, she may compete in subsequent races without changes to the boat, but shall be disqualified if she fails to appeal or the appeal is decided against her.

(d)   Measurement costs arising from a *protest* involving a measurement rule shall be paid by the unsuccessful *party* unless the protest committee decides otherwise.

65   INFORMING THE PARTIES AND OTHERS

65.1   After making its decision, the protest committee shall promptly inform the *parties* to the hearing of the facts found, the applicable *rules*, the decision, the reasons for it, and any penalties imposed or redress given.

65.2   A *party* to the hearing is entitled to receive the above information in writing, provided she asks for it in writing from the protest committee no later than seven days after being informed of the decision. The committee shall then promptly provide the information, including, when relevant, a diagram of the incident prepared or endorsed by the committee.

65.3   When the protest committee penalizes a boat under a measurement rule, it shall send the above information to the relevant measurement authorities.

66   REOPENING A HEARING

The protest committee may reopen a hearing when it decides that it may have made a significant error, or when significant new evidence becomes available within a reasonable time. It shall reopen a hearing when required by the national authority under rule F5. A *party* to the hearing may ask for a reopening no later than 24 hours after being informed of the decision. When a hearing is reopened, a majority of the members of the protest committee shall, if possible, be members of the original protest committee.

67   RULE 42 AND HEARING REQUIREMENT

When so stated in the sailing instructions, the protest committee may penalize without a hearing a boat that has broken rule 42, provided that a member of the committee or its designated observer has seen the incident, and a disqualification under this rule shall not be excluded from the boat's series score. A boat so penalized shall be informed by notification in the race results.

68   DAMAGES

The question of damages arising from a breach of any *rule* shall be governed by the prescriptions, if any, of the national authority.

Section C – Gross Misconduct

69   ALLEGATIONS OF GROSS MISCONDUCT

69.1   Action by a Protest Committee

(a)   When a protest committee, from its own observation or a report received from any source, believes that a competitor may have committed a gross breach of a *rule*, good manners or sportsmanship, or may have brought the sport into disrepute, it may call a hearing. The protest committee shall promptly inform the competitor in writing of the alleged misconduct and of the time and place of the hearing. If the competitor provides good reason for being unable to attend the hearing, the protest committee shall reschedule it.

(b)   A protest committee of at least three members shall conduct the hearing, following the procedures in rules 63.2, 63.3(a), 63.4 and 63.6. If it decides that the competitor committed the alleged misconduct it shall either
  (1)   warn the competitor or
  (2)   impose a penalty by excluding the competitor and, when appropriate, disqualifying a boat, from a race or the remaining races or all races of the series, or by taking other action within its jurisdiction. A disqualification under this rule shall not be excluded from the boat's series score.

(c)   The protest committee shall promptly report a penalty, but not a warning, to the national authorities of the venue, of the competitor and of the boat owner. If the protest committee is an international jury appointed by the ISAF under rule 89.2(b), it shall send a copy of the report to the ISAF.

(d)   If the competitor does not provide good reason for being unable to attend the hearing and does not come to it, the protest committee may conduct it without the competitor present. If the committee does so and penalizes the competitor, it shall include in the report it makes under rule 69.1(c) the facts found, the decision and the reasons for it.

(e)   If the protest committee chooses not to conduct the hearing without the competitor present or if the hearing cannot be scheduled for a time and place when it would be reasonable for the competitor to attend, the protest committee shall collect all available information and, if the allegation seems justified, make a report to the relevant national authorities. If the protest committee is an international jury appointed by the ISAF under rule 89.2(b), it shall send a copy of the report to the ISAF.

(f) When the protest committee has left the event and a report alleging misconduct is received, the race committee or organizing authority may appoint a new protest committee to proceed under this rule.

69.2 Action by a National Authority or Initial Action by the ISAF

(a) When a national authority or the ISAF receives a report alleging a gross breach of a *rule*, good manners or sportsmanship, a report alleging conduct that has brought the sport into disrepute, or a report required by rule 69.1(c) or 69.1(e), it may conduct an investigation and, when appropriate, shall conduct a hearing. It may then take any disciplinary action within its jurisdiction it considers appropriate against the competitor or boat, or other person involved, including suspending eligibility, permanently or for a specified period of time, to compete in any event held within its jurisdiction, and suspending ISAF eligibility under ISAF Regulation 19.

(b) The national authority of a competitor shall also suspend the ISAF eligibility of the competitor as required in ISAF Regulation 19.

(c) The national authority shall promptly report a suspension of eligibility under rule 69.2(a) to the ISAF, and to the national authorities of the person or the owner of the boat suspended if they are not members of the suspending national authority.

69.3 Subsequent Action by the ISAF

Upon receipt of a report required by rule 69.2(c) or ISAF Regulation 19, or following its own action under rule 69.2(a), the ISAF shall inform all national authorities, which may also suspend eligibility for events held within their jurisdiction. The ISAF Executive Committee shall suspend the competitor's ISAF eligibility as required in ISAF Regulation 19 if the competitor's national authority does not do so.

Section D – Appeals

70   **APPEALS AND REQUESTS TO A NATIONAL AUTHORITY**

70.1   Provided that the right of appeal has not been denied under rule 70.5, a *party* to a hearing may appeal a protest committee's decision or its procedures, but not the facts found.

70.2   A protest committee may request confirmation or correction of its decision.

70.3   An appeal under rule 70.1 or a request by a protest committee under rule 70.2 shall be sent to the national authority with which the organizing authority is associated under rule 89.1. However, if boats will pass through the waters of more than one national authority while *racing*, the sailing instructions shall identify the national authority to which appeals or requests may be sent.

70.4   A club or other organization affiliated to a national authority may request an interpretation of the *rules*, provided that no *protest* or request for redress that may be appealed is involved. The interpretation shall not be used for changing a previous protest committee decision.

70.5   There shall be no appeal from the decisions of an international jury constituted in compliance with Appendix N. Furthermore, if the notice of race and the sailing instructions so state, the right of appeal may be denied provided that

(a)   it is essential to determine promptly the result of a race that will qualify a boat to compete in a later stage of an event or a subsequent event (a national authority may prescribe that its approval is required for such a procedure);

(b)   a national authority so approves for a particular event open only to entrants under its own jurisdiction; or

(c)   a national authority after consultation with the ISAF so approves for a particular event, provided the protest committee is constituted as required by Appendix N, except that only two members of the protest committee need be International Judges.

70.6   Appeals and requests shall conform to Appendix F.

71 **NATIONAL AUTHORITY DECISIONS**

71.1 No *interested party* or member of the protest committee shall take any part in the discussion or decision on an appeal or a request for confirmation or correction.

71.2 The national authority may uphold, change or reverse the protest committee's decision; declare the *protest* or request for redress invalid; or return the *protest* or request for the hearing to be reopened, or for a new hearing and decision by the same or a different protest committee.

71.3 When from the facts found by the protest committee the national authority decides that a boat that was a *party* to a protest hearing broke a *rule*, it shall penalize her, whether or not that boat or that *rule* was mentioned in the protest committee's decision.

71.4 The decision of the national authority shall be final. The national authority shall send its decision in writing to all *parties* to the hearing and the protest committee, who shall be bound by the decision.

PART 6 – ENTRY & QUALIFICATION

75 **ENTERING A RACE**

75.1 To enter a race, a boat shall comply with the requirements of the organizing authority of the race. She shall be entered by

(a) a member of a club or other organization affiliated to an ISAF member national authority,
(b) such a club or organization, or
(c) a member of an ISAF member national authority.

75.2 Competitors shall comply with ISAF Regulation 19, Eligibility Code.

76 **EXCLUSION OF BOATS OR COMPETITORS**

76.1   The organizing authority or the race committee may reject or cancel the entry of a boat or exclude a competitor, subject to rule 76.2, provided it does so before the start of the first race and states the reason for doing so. However, the organizing authority or the race committee shall not reject or cancel the entry of a boat or exclude a competitor because of advertising, provided the boat or competitor complies with ISAF Regulation 20, Advertising Code.

76.2   At world and continental championships no entry within stated quotas shall be rejected or cancelled without first obtaining the approval of the relevant international class association (or the Offshore Racing Council) or the ISAF.

77   **IDENTIFICATION ON SAILS**
A boat shall comply with the requirements of Appendix G governing class insignia, national letters and numbers on sails.

78   **COMPLIANCE WITH CLASS RULES; CERTIFICATES**

78.1   A boat's owner and any other person in charge shall ensure that the boat is maintained to comply with her class rules and that her measurement or rating certificate, if any, remains valid.

78.2   When a *rule* requires a certificate to be produced before a boat *races*, and it is not produced, the boat may *race* provided that the race committee receives a statement signed by the person in charge that a valid certificate exists and that it will be given to the race committee before the end of the event. If the certificate is not received in time, the boat shall be disqualified from all races of the event.

78.3   When an equipment inspector or a measurer for an event decides that a boat or personal equipment does not comply with the class rules, he shall report the matter in writing to the race committee.

79   **CLASSIFICATION**
If the notice of race or class rules state that some or all competitors must satisfy classification requirements, the classification shall be carried out as described in ISAF Regulation 22, Sailor Classification Code.

80 ADVERTISING

A boat and her crew shall comply with ISAF Regulation 20, Advertising Code.

81 RESCHEDULED RACES

When a race has been rescheduled, all boats entered in the original race shall be notified. New entries that meet the entry requirements of the original race may be accepted at the discretion of the race committee.

PART 7 – RACE ORGANIZATION

85 GOVERNING RULES

The organizing authority, race committee and protest committee shall be governed by the *rules* in the conduct and judging of races.

86 CHANGES TO THE RACING RULES

86.1 A racing rule shall not be changed unless permitted in the rule itself or as follows:

(a) Prescriptions of a national authority may change a racing rule, but not the Definitions; a rule in the Introduction; Sportsmanship and the Rules; Part 1, 2 or 7; rule 42, 43, 69, 70, 71, 75, 76.2, 79 or 80; a rule of an appendix that changes one of these rules; Appendix H or N; or ISAF Regulation 19, 20, 21 or 22.

(b) Sailing instructions may change a racing rule, but not rule 76.1, Appendix F, or a rule listed in rule 86.1(a). However, the sailing instructions may change to 'two' or 'four' the number of hull lengths determining the *zone* around *marks*, provided that the number is the same for all *marks* and all boats using those *marks*. If the sailing instructions change a rule or that definition, they shall refer specifically to the rule or definition and state the change.

(c) Class rules may change only racing rules 42, 49, 50, 51, 52, 53 and 54. Such changes shall refer specifically to the rule and state the change.

Note: The second sentence of this rule takes effect on 1 January 2011.

86.2   In exception to rule 86.1, the ISAF may in limited circumstances (see ISAF Regulation 31.1.3) authorize changes to the racing rules for a specific international event. The authorization shall be stated in a letter of approval to the event organizing authority and in the notice of race and sailing instructions, and the letter shall be posted on the event's official notice board.

86.3   If a national authority so prescribes, the restrictions in rule 86.1 do not apply if rules are changed to develop or test proposed rules. The national authority may prescribe that its approval is required for such changes.

87   CHANGES TO CLASS RULES
The sailing instructions may change a class rule only when the class rules permit the change, or when written permission of the class association for the change is displayed on the official notice board.

88   NATIONAL PRESCRIPTIONS

88.1   The prescriptions that apply to an event are the prescriptions of the national authority with which the organizing authority is associated under rule 89.1. However, if boats will pass through the waters of more than one national authority while *racing*, the sailing instructions shall identify any other prescriptions that will apply and when they will apply.

88.2   The sailing instructions may change a prescription. However, a national authority may restrict changes to its prescriptions with a prescription to this rule, provided the ISAF approves its application to do so. The restricted prescriptions shall not be changed by the sailing instructions.

89   ORGANIZING AUTHORITY; NOTICE OF RACE; APPOINTMENT OF RACE OFFICIALS

89.1   Organizing Authority
Races shall be organized by an organizing authority, which shall be

(a) the ISAF;

(b) a member national authority of the ISAF;

(c) a club or other organization affiliated to a national authority;

(d) a class association, either with the approval of a national authority or in conjunction with an affiliated club;

(e) an unaffiliated body in conjunction with an affiliated club where the body is owned and controlled by the club. The national authority of the club may prescribe that its approval is required for such an event; or

(f) if approved by the ISAF and the national authority of the club, an unaffiliated body in conjunction with an affiliated club where the body is not owned and controlled by the club.

89.2 Notice of Race; Appointment of Race Officials

(a) The organizing authority shall publish a notice of race that conforms to rule J1. The notice of race may be changed provided adequate notice is given.

(b) The organizing authority shall appoint a race committee and, when appropriate, appoint a protest committee and umpires. However, the race committee, an international jury and umpires may be appointed by the ISAF as provided in the ISAF regulations.

90 RACE COMMITTEE; SAILING INSTRUCTIONS; SCORING

90.1 Race Committee

The race committee shall conduct races as directed by the organizing authority and as required by the *rules*.

90.2 Sailing Instructions

(a) The race committee shall publish written sailing instructions that conform to rule J2.

(b) When appropriate, for an event where entries from other countries are expected, the sailing instructions shall include, in English, the applicable national prescriptions.

(c) Changes to the sailing instructions shall be in writing and posted on the official notice board before the time stated in the sailing instructions or, on the water, communicated to each boat before her warning signal. Oral changes may be given only on the water, and only if the procedure is stated in the sailing instructions.

90.3   **Scoring**

(a)   The race committee shall score a race or series as provided in Appendix A using the Low Point System, unless the sailing instructions specify the Bonus Point System or some other system. A race shall be scored if it is not *abandoned* and if one boat sails the course in compliance with rule 28.1 and *finishes* within the time limit, if any, even if she retires after *finishing* or is disqualified.

(b)   When a scoring system provides for excluding one or more race scores from a boat's series score, the score for disqualification under rule 2; rule 30.3's last sentence; rule 42 if rule 67, P2.2 or P2.3 applies; or rule 69.1(b)(2) shall not be excluded. The next-worse score shall be excluded instead.

91   **PROTEST COMMITTEE**

A protest committee shall be

(a)   a committee appointed by the organizing authority or race committee, or

(b)   an international jury appointed by the organizing authority or as prescribed in the ISAF regulations and meeting the requirements of Appendix N. A national authority may prescribe that its approval is required for the appointment of international juries for races within its jurisdiction, except ISAF events or when international juries are appointed by the ISAF under rule 89.2(b).

APPENDIX A – SCORING

See rule 90.3.

A1   **NUMBER OF RACES**

The number of races scheduled and the number required to be completed to constitute a series shall be stated in the sailing instructions.

A2   **SERIES SCORES**

Each boat's series score shall be the total of her race scores excluding her worst score. (The sailing instructions may make a different arrangement by providing, for example, that no score will be excluded, that two or more scores will be excluded, or that a specified number of scores will be excluded if a specified number of races are completed. A race is completed if scored; see rule 90.3(a).) If a boat has two or more equal worst scores, the score(s) for the race(s) sailed earliest in the series shall be excluded. The boat with the lowest series score wins and others shall be ranked accordingly.

A3 STARTING TIMES AND FINISHING PLACES

The time of a boat's starting signal shall be her starting time, and the order in which boats *finish* a race shall determine their finishing places. However, when a handicap or rating system is used a boat's corrected time shall determine her finishing place.

A4 LOW POINT AND BONUS POINT SYSTEMS

Most series are scored using either the Low Point System or the Bonus Point System. The Low Point System uses a boat's finishing place as her race score. The Bonus Point System benefits the first six finishers because of the greater difficulty in advancing from fourth place to third, for example, than from fourteenth place to thirteenth. The Low Point System will apply unless the sailing instructions specify another system; see rule 90.3(a). If the Bonus Point System is chosen it can be made to apply by stating in the sailing instructions that 'The Bonus Point System of Appendix A will apply.'

A4.1 Each boat *starting* and *finishing* and not thereafter retiring, being penalized or given redress shall be scored points as follows:

Finishing place	Low Point System	Bonus Point System
First	1	0
Second	2	3
Third	3	5.7
Fourth	4	8
Fifth	5	10
Sixth	6	11.7
Seventh	7	13
Each place thereafter	Add 1 point	Add 1 point

A4.2   A boat that did not *start*, did not *finish*, retired after *finishing* or was disqualified shall be scored points for the finishing place one more than the number of boats entered in the series. A boat that is penalized under rule 30.2 or that takes a penalty under rule 44.3(a) shall be scored points as provided in rule 44.3(c).

A5   **SCORES DETERMINED BY THE RACE COMMITTEE**
A boat that did not *start*, comply with rule 30.2 or 30.3, or *finish*, or that takes a penalty under rule 44.3(a) or retires after *finishing*, shall be scored accordingly by the race committee without a hearing. Only the protest committee may take other scoring actions that worsen a boat's score.

A6   **CHANGES IN PLACES AND SCORES OF OTHER BOATS**

A6.1   If a boat is disqualified from a race or retires after *finishing*, each boat with a worse finishing place shall be moved up one place.

A6.2   If the protest committee decides to give redress by adjusting a boat's score, the scores of other boats shall not be changed unless the protest committee decides otherwise.

A7   **RACE TIES**
If boats are tied at the finishing line or if a handicap or rating system is used and boats have equal corrected times, the points for the place for which the boats have tied and for the place(s) immediately below shall be added together and divided equally. Boats tied for a race prize shall share it or be given equal prizes.

A8   **SERIES TIES**

A8.1   If there is a series-score tie between two or more boats, each boat's race scores shall be listed in order of best to worst, and at the first point(s) where there is a difference the tie shall be broken in favour of the boat(s) with the best score(s). No excluded scores shall be used.

A8.2   If a tie remains between two or more boats, they shall be ranked in order of their scores in the last race. Any remaining ties shall be broken by using the tied boats' scores in the next-to-last race and so on until all ties are broken. These scores shall be used even if some of them are excluded scores.

A9   RACE SCORES IN A SERIES LONGER THAN A REGATTA

For a series that is held over a period of time longer than a regatta, a boat that came to the starting area but did not *start*, did not *finish*, retired after *finishing* or was disqualified shall be scored points for the finishing place one more than the number of boats that came to the starting area. A boat that did not come to the starting area shall be scored points for the finishing place one more than the number of boats entered in the series.

A10   GUIDANCE ON REDRESS

If the protest committee decides to give redress by adjusting a boat's score for a race, it is advised to consider scoring her

(a)   points equal to the average, to the nearest tenth of a point (0.05 to be rounded upward), of her points in all the races in the series except the race in question;

(b)   points equal to the average, to the nearest tenth of a point (0.05 to be rounded upward), of her points in all the races before the race in question; or

(c)   points based on the position of the boat in the race at the time of the incident that justified redress.

A11   SCORING ABBREVIATIONS

These scoring abbreviations shall be used for recording the circumstances described:

DNC   Did not *start*; did not come to the starting area

DNS   Did not *start* (other than DNC and OCS)

OCS   Did not *start*; on the course side of the starting line at her starting signal and failed to *start*, or broke rule 30.1

ZFP   20% penalty under rule 30.2

BFD   Disqualification under rule 30.3

SCP   Took a Scoring Penalty under rule 44.3(a)

DNF   Did not *finish*

RAF   Retired after *finishing*

DSQ   Disqualification

DNE   Disqualification (other than DGM) not excludable under rule 90.3(b)

DGM   Disqualification for gross misconduct not excludable under rule 90.3(b)

RDG   Redress given

APPENDIX B – WINDSURFING COMPETITION RULES

Windsurfing competition shall be sailed under The Racing Rules of Sailing *as changed by this appendix. The term 'boat' elsewhere in the racing rules means 'board' or 'boat' as appropriate. A windsurfing event can include one or more of the following disciplines or their formats:*

Discipline	Formats
Racing	*Course racing; slalom; marathon*
Expression	*Wave performance; freestyle*
Speed	

In expression competition a board's performance is judged on skill and variety rather than speed and is organized using elimination series. Either wave performance or freestyle competition is organized, depending on the wave conditions at the venue. In speed competition, a 'round' consists of one or more speed runs in which the boards take turns sailing the course at intervals. In the racing discipline a marathon race is a race scheduled to last more than one hour.

In racing or expression competition, 'heat' means one elimination contest, a 'round' consists of one or more heats, and an elimination series consists of one or more rounds.

B1 DEFINITIONS

B1.1 The following additional definitions apply:

About to Round or Pass
> A board is *about to round or pass a mark* when her *proper course* is to begin to manoeuvre to round or pass it.

Beach Start When the starting line is on the beach, or so close to the beach that the competitor must stand in the water to *start*, the start is a *beach start*.

Capsized A board is *capsized* when her sail or the competitor is in the water.

B1.2 The following definitions apply only to expression competition:

Coming In and Going Out

A board sailing in the same direction as the incoming surf is *coming in*. A board sailing in the direction opposite to the incoming surf is *going out*.

Jumping A board is *jumping* when she takes off at the top of a wave while *going out*.

Overtaking A board is *overtaking* from the moment she gains an *overlap* from *clear astern* until the moment she is *clear ahead* of the *overtaken* board.

Possession The first board sailing shoreward immediately in front of a wave has *possession* of that wave. However, when it is impossible to determine which board is first the *windward* board has possession.

Recovering A board is *recovering* from the time her sail or, when water-starting, the competitor is out of the water until she has steerage way.

Surfing A board is *surfing* when she is on or immediately in front of a wave while *coming in*.

Transition A board changing *tacks*, or taking off while *coming in*, or one that is not *surfing*, *jumping*, *capsized* or *recovering* is in *transition*.

B2 RULES FOR ALL COMPETITION

Rule B2 applies to all competition.

B2.1 Changes to the Rules of Part 4

(a) Rule 42 is changed to 'A board shall be propelled only by the action of the wind on the sail, by the action of the water on the hull and by the unassisted actions of the competitor.'

(b) Add to rule 43.1(a): 'However, a competitor may wear a drinking container that shall have a capacity of at least one litre and weigh no more than 1.5 kilograms when full.'

(c)   Rule 44.2 is changed so that two turns are replaced by one 360° turn with no requirement for tacks or gybes.

(d)   Add to rule 47.1: 'except as stated in rule 41.2'. (See rule B4.4.)

B2.2   Entry and Qualification

Add to rule 78.1: 'When so prescribed by the ISAF, a numbered and dated device on a board and her centreboard, fin and rig shall serve as her measurement certificate.'

B2.3   Event Organization

(a)   The last sentence of rule 90.2(c) is deleted.

(b)   Add new rule 90.2(d): 'Oral instructions may be given only if the procedure is stated in the sailing instructions.'

B2.4   Identification on Sails

(a)   Add to rule G1.1(a): 'The insignia shall not refer to anything other than the manufacturer or class and shall not consist of more than two letters and three numbers or an abstract design.'

(b)   Rules G1.3(a), G1.3(c), G1.3(d) and G1.3(e) are changed to

> The class insignia shall be displayed once on each side of the sail in the area above a line projected at right angles from a point on the luff of the sail one-third of the distance from the head to the wishbone. The national letters and sail numbers shall be in the central third of that part of the sail above the wishbone, clearly separated from any advertising. They shall be black and applied back to back on an opaque white background. The background shall extend a minimum of 30 mm beyond the characters. Between the national letters and sail number a '–' and normal spacing shall be applied.

B2.5   Touching a Mark

Rule 31 is changed to 'A board may touch a *mark* but shall not hold on to it.'

B2.6   Deleted Rules

Rules 17, 18.3, 43.2, 44.3, 45, 47.2, 48, 49, 50, 51, 52, 54, 61.1(a)(2), 67, J2.2(28) and J2.2(33) are deleted.

B3   **RULES FOR RACING COMPETITION**
Rule B 3 applies to racing competition. Rule B2 also applies.

B3.1   **Changes to the Rules of Part 2, Section C**

(a)   The first sentence of rule 18.1 is changed to 'Rule 18 applies between boards when they are required to leave a *mark* on the same side and at least one of them is *about to round or pass* it.'

(b)   Rule 18.2(b) is changed to
If boards are *overlapped* when the first of them is *about to round or pass* the *mark*, the outside board at that moment shall thereafter give the inside board *Mark-Room*. If a board is *clear ahead* when she is *about to round or pass* the *mark*, the board *clear astern* at that moment shall thereafter give her *Mark-Room*.

(c)   Rule 18.2(c) is changed to
When a board is required to give *Mark-Room* by rule 18.2(b), she shall continue to do so even if later an *overlap* is broken or a new *overlap* begins. However, if either board passes head to wind rule 18.2(b) ceases to apply.

(d)   Rule 18.4 is changed to
When an inside *overlapped* right-of-way board must gybe or bear away at a *mark* to sail her *proper course*, until she gybes or bears away she shall sail no farther from the *mark* than needed to sail that course. Rule 18.4 does not apply at a gate *mark*.

B3.2   **Changes to Other Rules of Part 2**

(a)   In the preamble of Part 2, 'rule 23.1' is changed to 'rules 23.1 and 23.3'.

(b)   Add new rule 16.3:
In slalom racing, a right-of-way board shall not change course during the last 30 seconds before her starting signal if as a result the other board would have to take immediate action to avoid contact.

(c)   Rule 22 becomes rule 22.1 and its last sentence is deleted. Add new rule 22.2: 'A *capsized* board shall not take an action that hinders another board.'

(d)   Rule 23.1 is changed to 'If reasonably possible, a board not *racing* shall not interfere with a board that is *racing*. After *finishing*, a board shall immediately clear the finishing line and *marks* and avoid boards still *racing*.'

(e) Add new rule 23.3: 'A board shall not sail in the course area defined in the sailing instructions when races are taking place except in her own race.'

(f) Add new rule 24:

24 SAIL OUT OF THE WATER WHEN STARTING

When approaching the starting line to *start*, a board shall have her sail out of the water and in a normal position, except when accidentally *capsized*.

B3.3 **Starting Races**

The sailing instructions shall specify one of these starting systems.

(a) SYSTEM 1

See rule 26, Starting Races.

(b) SYSTEM 2

Races shall be started by using the following signals. Times shall be taken from the visual signals; the absence of a sound signal shall be disregarded.

Signal	Flag and sound	Minutes before starting signal
Attention	Class flag or heat number	3
Warning	Red flag; attention signal removed; 1 sound	2
Preparatory	Yellow flag; Red flag removed; 1 sound	1
	Yellow flag removed	1/2
Starting	Green flag; 1 sound	0

(c) SYSTEM 3 (FOR BEACH STARTS)

(1) Before her start each board in a heat or class shall draw a number for her station on the starting line. The stations shall be numbered so that station 1 is the most windward one.

(2) After boards have been called to take their positions, the race committee shall make the preparatory signal by displaying a red flag with one sound. The starting signal shall be made, at any time after the preparatory signal, by removing the red flag with one sound.

(3) After the starting signal each board shall take the shortest route from her starting station to her windsurfing position in the water (with both of the competitor's feet on the board).

B3.4 **Other Rules for the Conduct of a Race**
Add new rule 29.3:

29.3 Recall for a Slalom Race

(a) When at a board's starting signal for a slalom race or heat any part of her hull, crew or equipment is on the course side of the starting line, the race committee shall signal a general recall.

(b) If the race committee acts under rule 29.3(a) and the board is identified, she shall be disqualified without a hearing, even if the race or heat is *abandoned*. The race committee shall hail or display her sail number, and she shall leave the course area immediately. If the race or heat is restarted or resailed, she shall not sail in it.

(c) If a slalom race or heat was completed but was later *abandoned* by the protest committee and if the race or heat is resailed, a board disqualified under rule 29.3(b) may sail in it.

B4 RULES FOR EXPRESSION COMPETITION

B4.1 **Right-of-Way Rules**
These rules replace all rules of Part 2.

(a) COMING IN AND GOING OUT
A board *coming in* shall *keep clear* of a board *going out*. When two boards are *going out* or *coming in* while on the same wave, or when neither is *going out* or *coming in*, a board on *port tack* shall *keep clear* of one on *starboard tack*.

(b) BOARDS ON THE SAME WAVE, COMING IN
When two or more boards are on a wave *coming in*, a board that does not have *possession* shall *keep clear*.

(c) CLEAR ASTERN, CLEAR AHEAD AND OVERTAKING
A board *clear astern* and not on a wave shall *keep clear* of a board *clear ahead*. An *overtaking* board that is not on a wave shall *keep clear*.

(d) TRANSITION
A board in *transition* shall *keep clear* of one that is not.

When two boards are in *transition* at the same time, the one on the other's port side or the one astern shall *keep clear*.

B4.2   Starting and Ending Heats

Heats shall be started and ended by using the following signals:

(a)   STARTING A HEAT
Each flag shall be removed when the next flag is displayed.

Signal	Flag and sound	Minutes before starting signal
Attention	Heat number	3
Warning	Red flag; 1 sound	2
Preparatory	Yellow flag; 1 sound	1
Starting	Green flag; 1 sound	0

(b)   ENDING A HEAT

Signal	Flag and sound	Minutes before ending signal
End warning	Green flag removed; 1 sound	1
Ending	Red flag; 1 sound	0

B4.3   Registration of Sails; Course Area; Heat Duration

(a)   Boards shall register with the race committee the colours and other particulars of their sails, or their identification according to another method stated in the sailing instructions, no later than the starting signal for the heat two heats before their own.

(b)   The course area shall be defined in the sailing instructions and posted on the official notice board no later than 10 minutes before the starting signal for the first heat. A board shall be scored only while sailing in the course area.

(c)   Any change in heat duration shall be announced by the race committee no later than 15 minutes before the starting signal for the first heat in the next round.

B4.4 Outside Help

Rule 41 becomes rule 41.1. Add new rule 41.2:

> An assistant may provide replacement equipment to a board but shall keep clear of other boards competing. A board whose assistant fails to keep clear shall be penalized. The penalty shall be at the discretion of the protest committee.

B5 ELIMINATION SERIES

Rule B5 applies when an elimination series is organized in which boards compete in heats.

B5.1 Elimination Series Procedure

(a) Competition shall take the form of one or more elimination series. Each of them shall consist of either a maximum of four rounds in a single elimination series where only a number of the best scorers advance, or a maximum of ten rounds in a double elimination series where boards have more than one opportunity to advance.

(b) Boards shall sail one against another in pairs, or in groups determined by the elimination ladder. The selected form of competition shall not be changed while a round remains uncompleted.

B5.2 Seeding and Ranking Lists

(a) When a seeding or ranking list is used to establish the heats of the first round, places 1–8 (four heats) or 1–16 (eight heats) shall be distributed evenly among the heats.

(b) For a subsequent elimination series, if any, boards shall be reassigned to new heats according to the ranking in the previous elimination series.

(c) The organizing authority's seeding decisions are final and are not grounds for a request for redress.

B5.3 Heat Schedule

The schedule of heats shall be posted on the official notice board no later than 30 minutes before the starting signal for the first heat.

B5.4 Advancement and Byes

(a) In racing and expression competition, the boards in each heat to advance to the next round shall be announced by the race committee no later than 10 minutes before the starting signal for the first heat. The number advancing may be changed by the protest committee as a result of a redress decision.

(b) In expression competition, any first-round byes shall be assigned to the highest-seeded boards.

(c) In wave performance competition, only the winner of each heat shall advance to the next round.

(d) In freestyle competition, boards shall advance to the next round as follows: from an eight-board heat, the best four advance, and the winner will sail against the fourth and the second against the third; from a four-board heat, the best two advance and will sail against each other.

B5.5 Finals

(a) The final shall consist of a maximum of three races. The race committee shall announce the number of races to be sailed in the final no later than five minutes before the warning signal for the first final race.

(b) A runners-up final may be sailed after the final. All boards in the semifinal heats that failed to qualify for the final may compete in it.

B6 RULES FOR SPEED COMPETITION

B6.1 General Rules

All rules of Part 2 are replaced by relevant parts of this rule.

(a) BEACH AND WATER STARTING
A board shall not *beach start* or water start on the course or in the starting area, except to sail off the course to avoid boards that are *starting* or *racing*.

(b) LEAVING THE COURSE AREA
A board leaving the course area shall *keep clear* of boards *racing*.

(c) COURSE CONTROL
When the race committee points an orange flag at a board, she shall immediately leave the course area.

(d) RETURNING TO THE STARTING AREA
A board returning to the starting area shall keep clear of the course.

(e) RUN; ROUND
The maximum number of runs to be made by each board

in a round shall be announced by the race committee no later than 15 minutes before the starting signal for the first round.

(f) DURATION OF A ROUND

The duration of a round shall be announced by the race committee no later than 15 minutes before the starting signal for the next round.

(g) CONDITIONS FOR ESTABLISHING A RECORD

The minimum distance for a world record is 500 metres. Other records may be established over shorter distances. The course shall be defined by posts and transits ashore or by buoys afloat. Transits shall not converge.

B6.2 Starting System for Speed Competition

Rounds shall be started and ended by using the following signals. Each flag shall be removed when the next flag is displayed.

(a) STARTING A ROUND

Signal	Flag	Meaning
Stand-by	Red flag	Course closed
Course closed	AP and red flag	Course closed; will open shortly
Preparatory	Yellow flag	Course will open in 5 minutes
Starting	Green flag	Course is open

(b) ENDING A ROUND

Signal	Flag	Meaning
End warning	Green and yellow flag	Course will be closed in 5 minutes
Extension	Green flag and L	Current round extended by 15 minutes
Round ended	Red flag and L	A new round will be started shortly

B6.3 **Penalties**

(a) If a board fails to comply with a warning by the race committee, she may be cautioned and her sail number shall be posted on a notice board near the finishing line.

(b) If a board is cautioned a second time during the same round, she shall be suspended by the race committee from the remainder of the round and her sail number shall be posted on the official notice board.

(c) A board observed in the course area while suspended shall be excluded from the competition without a hear-ing and none of her previous times or results shall be valid.

(d) Any breach of the verification rules may result in a suspension from the competition for any period.

B6.4 **Verification**

(a) An observer appointed by the World Sailing Speed Record Council (WSSRC) shall be present and verify run times and speeds at world record attempts. The race committee shall verify run times and speeds at other record attempts.

(b) A competitor shall not enter the timing control area or discuss any timing matter directly with the timing organization. Any timing question shall be directed to the race committee.

B7 **PROTESTS, REDRESS, HEARINGS AND APPEALS**

B7.1 The first three sentences of rule 61.1(a) are replaced by
A board intending to protest shall inform the other board at the first reasonable opportunity. When her *protest* concerns an incident in the racing area that she is involved in or sees, she shall hail 'Protest'. She shall inform the race committee of her intention to protest immediately after she *finishes* or retires.

B7.2 In an elimination series, *protests* and requests for redress shall be made orally immediately following the heat in which the incident occurred. The protest committee may take evidence in any way it considers appropriate and may communicate its decision orally.

B7.3 Add new rule 62.1(e): 'a board that failed to *keep clear* and caused *capsize* of the other board.'

B7.4 Add new rule 70.7: 'Appeals are not permitted in disciplines with elimination series.'

B8   SCORING

B8.1   Overall Scores

If an event includes more than one discipline or format the sailing instructions shall state how the overall score is to be calculated.

B8.2   Series Scores

Rule A2 is changed to

Each board's series score shall be the total of her race, elimination series or speed round scores with the number of her worst scores excluded as follows:

Course races	speed rounds	Slalom and expression elimination series	Number excluded
1–4	1–3	1–2	0
5–11	4–6	3–4	1
12 or more	7–10	5–7	2
	11–15	8 or more	3
	16 or more		4

If a board has two or more equal worst scores, the score(s) for the race(s) sailed earliest in the series shall be excluded. The board with the lowest series score wins and others shall be ranked accordingly. Rules B8.5, B8.6 and B8.7 contain exceptions to this rule.

B8.3   Scoring Systems

Add to the end of the first sentence of rule A4.2: 'or, in an elimination series, the number of boards in that heat'.

B8.4   Uncompleted Heat

When a heat cannot be completed, the points for the unscored places shall be added together and divided by the number of places in that heat. The resulting number of points, to the nearest tenth of a point (0.05 to be rounded upward), shall be given to each board entered in the heat.

B8.5   Scoring a Final Series in Slalom Racing

(a)   If three final races are completed, a board's series score in the final shall be the total of her race scores excluding her worst score. Otherwise her series score shall be the total of her race scores.

(b) A board that did not *start*, did not *finish*, retired after *finishing* or was disqualified from a final race shall be scored points equal to the total number of boards entered in the final.

B8.6 Expression Competition Scoring

(a) Expression competition shall be scored by a panel of three judges. However, the panel may have a greater odd number of members, and there may be two such panels. Each judge shall give points for each manoeuvre based on the scale stated in the sailing instructions.

(b) The criteria of scoring shall be decided by the race committee and announced on the official notice board no later than 30 minutes before the starting signal for the first heat.

(c) A board's heat standing shall be determined by adding together the points given by each judge. The board with the highest score wins and others shall be ranked accordingly.

(d) Both semifinal heats shall have been sailed for an elimination series to be valid.

(e) Except for members of the race committee responsible for scoring the event, only competitors in the heat shall be allowed to see judges' score sheets for the heat. Each score sheet shall bear the full name of the judge.

(f) Scoring decisions of the judges shall not be grounds for a request for redress by a board.

B8.7 Speed Competition

The speeds of a board's fastest two runs in a round shall be averaged to determine her standing in that round. The board with the highest average wins and others shall be ranked accordingly.

B8.8 Series Ties

(a) RACING AND SPEED COMPETITION

Rule A8 is changed as follows for racing and speed competition:

(1) Add new rule A8.1: 'If there is a series-score tie between two or more boards, it shall be broken in favour of the board(s) with the best single excluded race score(s).'

(2) Rule A8.1 becomes rule A8.2. Its beginning 'If there is a series-score tie' is changed to 'If a tie remains' and its last sentence is changed to 'These scores shall be used even if some of them are excluded scores.'

(3) Rule A8.2 becomes rule A8.3 and its beginning 'If a tie remains' is changed to 'If a tie still remains'.

(b) EXPRESSION COMPETITION

Rule A8 is changed as follows for expression competition:

(1) In a heat, if there is a tie in the total points given by one or more judges, it shall be broken in favour of the board with the higher single score in the priority category. If the categories are weighted equally, in wave performance competition the tie shall be broken in favour of the board with the higher single score in wave riding, and in freestyle competition in favour of the board with the higher score for overall impression. If a tie remains, in wave performance competition it shall be broken in favour of the board with the higher single score in the category without priority, and in freestyle competition it shall stand as the final result.

(2) If there is a tie in the series score, it shall be broken in favour of the board that scored better more times than the other board. All scores shall be used even if some of them are excluded scores.

(3) If a tie still remains, the heat shall be resailed. If this is not possible, the tie shall stand as the final result.

APPENDIX C – MATCH RACING RULES

Match races shall be sailed under The Racing Rules of Sailing *as changed by this appendix. Matches shall be umpired unless the notice of race and sailing instructions state otherwise.*

C1   TERMINOLOGY

'Competitor' means the skipper, team or boat as appropriate for the event. 'Flight' means two or more matches started in the same starting sequence.

C2 **CHANGES TO THE DEFINITIONS AND THE RULES OF PARTS 2 AND 4**

C2.1 The definition *Finish* is changed to

A boat *finishes* when any part of her hull, or crew or equipment in normal position, crosses the finishing line in the direction of the course from the last *mark* after completing any penalties. However, when penalties are cancelled under rule C7.2(d) after one or both boats have *finished* each shall be recorded as *finished* when she crossed the line.

C2.2 Add to the definition *Proper Course*: 'A boat taking a penalty or manoeuvring to take a penalty is not sailing a *proper course*.'

C2.3 In the definition *Zone* the distance is changed to two hull lengths.

C2.4 Rule 13 is changed to

13 WHILE TACKING OR GYBING

13.1 After a boat passes head to wind, she shall *keep clear* of other boats until she is on a close-hauled course.

13.2 After the foot of the mainsail of a boat sailing downwind crosses the centreline she shall *keep clear* of other boats until her mainsail has filled.

13.3 While rule 13.1 or 13.2 applies, rules 10, 11 and 12 do not. However, if two boats are subject to rule 13.1 or 13.2 at the same time, the one on the other's port side or the one astern shall *keep clear*.

C2.5 Rule 16.2 is deleted.

C2.6 Rule 18.3 is changed to

If two boats were on opposite *tacks* and one of them changes *tack* and as a result is subject to rule 13.1 in the *zone* when the other is *fetching* the *mark*, rule 18.2 does not thereafter apply. If, once the boat that changed *tack* has completed her tack,

(a) the other boat cannot by luffing avoid becoming *overlapped* inside her, she is entitled to *Mark-Room*, the boat that changed *tack* shall *keep clear* and rule 15 does not apply;

(b) the other boat can by luffing avoid becoming *overlapped* inside her, the boat that changed *tack* is entitled to *Mark-Room*.

C2.7 When rule 20 applies, the following arm signals by the helmsman are required in addition to the hails:

(a) for 'Room to tack', repeatedly and clearly pointing to windward; and

(b) for 'You tack', repeatedly and clearly pointing at the other boat and waving the arm to windward.

C2.8 Rule 23.1 is changed to 'If reasonably possible, a boat not *racing* shall not interfere with a boat that is *racing* or an umpire boat.'

C2.9 Add new rule 23.3: 'When boats in different matches meet, any change of course by either boat shall be consistent with complying with a *rule* or trying to win her own match.'

C2.10 Add to the preamble of Part 4: 'Rule 42 shall also apply between the warning and preparatory signals.'

C2.11 Rule 42.2(d) is changed to 'sculling: repeated movement of the helm to propel the boat forward;'

C3 **RACE SIGNALS AND CHANGES TO RELATED RULES**

C3.1 **Starting Signals**

The signals for starting a match shall be as follows. Times shall be taken from the visual signals; the failure of a sound signal shall be disregarded. If more than one match will be sailed, the starting signal for one match shall be the warning signal for the next match.

Time in minutes	Visual signal	Sound signal	Means
10	Flag F displayed	One	Attention signal
6	Flag F removed	None	
5	Numeral pennant displayed*	One	Warning signal
4	Flag P displayed	One	Preparatory signal
2	Blue or yellow flag or both displayed**	One**	End of pre-start entry time
0	Warning and preparatory signals removed	One	Starting signal

*Within a flight, numeral pennant 1 means Match 1, pennant 2 means Match 2, etc., unless the sailing instructions state otherwise.

**These signals shall be made only if one or both boats fail to comply with rule C4.2. The flag(s) shall be displayed until the umpires have signalled a penalty or for one minute, whichever is earlier.

C3.2 Changes to Related Rules

(a) Rule 29.1 is changed to

(1) When at a boat's starting signal any part of her hull, crew or equipment is on the course side of the starting line or one of its extensions, the race committee shall promptly display a blue or yellow flag identifying the boat with one sound. The flag shall be displayed until the boat is completely on the pre-start side of the starting line or one of its extensions or until two minutes after her starting signal, whichever is earlier.

(2) When at a boat's starting signal no part of her hull, crew or equipment is on the course side of the starting line or one of its extensions, and before she *starts* she sails to the course side across an extension, the race committee shall promptly display a blue or yellow flag identifying the boat. The flag shall be displayed until the boat is completely on the pre-start side of the starting line or one of its extensions or until two minutes after her starting signal, whichever is earlier.

(b) In the race signal AP the last sentence is changed to 'The attention signal will be made 1 minute after removal unless at that time the race is *postponed* again or *abandoned*.'

(c) In the race signal N the last sentence is changed to 'The attention signal will be made 1 minute after removal unless at that time the race is *abandoned* again or *postponed*.'

C3.3 Finishing Line Signals

The race signal Blue flag or shape shall not be used.

C4 REQUIREMENTS BEFORE THE START

C4.1 At her preparatory signal, each boat shall be outside the line

that is at a 90° angle to the starting line through the starting *mark* at her assigned end. In the race schedule pairing list, the boat listed on the left-hand side is assigned the port end and shall display a blue flag at her stern while *racing*. The other boat is assigned the starboard end and shall display a yellow flag at her stern while *racing*.

C4.2 Within the two-minute period following her preparatory signal, a boat shall cross and clear the starting line, the first time from the course side to the pre-start side.

C5   SIGNALS BY UMPIRES

C5.1 A green and white flag with one long sound means 'No penalty'.

C5.2 A blue or yellow flag identifying a boat with one long sound means 'The identified boat shall take a penalty by complying with rule C7.'

C5.3 A red flag with or soon after a blue or yellow flag with one long sound means 'The identified boat shall take a penalty by complying with rule C7.3(d).'

C5.4 A black flag with a blue or yellow flag and one long sound means 'The identified boat is disqualified, and the match is terminated and awarded to the other boat.'

C5.5 One short sound means 'A penalty is now completed.'

C5.6 Repetitive short sounds mean 'A boat is no longer taking a penalty and the penalty remains.'

C5.7 A blue or yellow flag or shape displayed from an umpire boat means 'The identified boat has an outstanding penalty.'

C6   PROTESTS AND REQUESTS FOR REDRESS BY BOATS

C6.1 A boat may protest another boat
  (a) under a rule of Part 2, except rule 14, by clearly displaying flag Y immediately after an incident in which she was involved;
  (b) under any rule not listed in rule C6.1(a) or C6.2 by clearly displaying a red flag as soon as possible after the incident.

C6.2 A boat may not protest another boat under
    (a) rule 14, unless damage or injury results;
    (b) a rule of Part 2, unless she was involved in the incident;
    (c) rule 31 or 42; or
    (d) rule C4 or C7.

C6.3 A boat intending to request redress because of circumstances that arise before she *finishes* or retires shall clearly display a red flag as soon as possible after she becomes aware of those circumstances, but no later than two minutes after *finishing* or retiring.

C6.4 (a) A boat protesting under rule C6.1(a) shall remove flag Y before or as soon as possible after the umpires' signal.
    (b) A boat protesting under rule C6.1(b) or requesting redress under rule C6.3 shall, for her *protest* or request to be valid, keep her red flag displayed until she has so informed the umpires after *finishing* or retiring. No written *protest* or request for redress is required.

C6.5 Umpire Decisions
    (a) After flag Y is displayed, the umpires shall decide whether to penalize any boat. They shall signal their decision in compliance with rule C5.1, C5.2 or C5.3.
    (b) The red-flag penalty in rule C5.3 shall be used when a boat has gained a controlling position as a result of breaking a *rule*, but the umpires are not certain that the conditions for an additional umpire-initiated penalty have been fulfilled.

C6.6 Protest Committee Decisions
    (a) The protest committee may take evidence in any way it considers appropriate and may communicate its decision orally.
    (b) If the protest committee decides that a breach of a *rule* has had no significant effect on the outcome of the match, it may
        (1) impose a penalty of one point or part of one point;
        (2) order a resail; or
        (3) make another arrangement it decides is equitable, which may be to impose no penalty.
    (c) The penalty for breaking rule 14 when damage or injury results will be at the discretion of the protest committee, and may include exclusion from further races in the event.

C7   PENALTY SYSTEM

C7.1   Deleted Rule
Rule 44 is deleted.

C7.2   All Penalties
(a)   A penalized boat may delay taking a penalty within the limitations of rule C7.3 and shall take it as follows:
  (1)   When on a leg of the course to a windward *mark*, she shall gybe and, as soon as reasonably possible, luff to a close-hauled course.
  (2)   When on a leg of the course to a leeward mark or the finishing line, she shall tack and, as soon as reasonably possible, bear away to a course that is more than ninety degrees from the true wind.

(b)   Add to rule 2: 'When *racing*, a boat need not take a penalty unless signalled to do so by an umpire.'

(c)   A boat completes a leg of the course when her bow crosses the extension of the line from the previous *mark* through the *mark* she is rounding, or on the last leg when she *finishes*.

(d)   A penalized boat shall not be recorded as having *finished* until she takes her penalty and sails completely to the course side of the line and then *finishes*, unless the penalty is cancelled before or after she crosses the finishing line.

(e)   If a boat has one or two outstanding penalties and the other boat in her match is penalized, one penalty for each boat shall be cancelled except that a red-flag penalty shall not cancel or be cancelled by another penalty.

(f)   If a boat has more than two outstanding penalties, the umpires shall signal her disqualification under rule C5.4.

C7.3   Penalty Limitations
(a)   A boat taking a penalty that includes a tack shall have the spinnaker head below the main-boom gooseneck from the time she passes head to wind until she is on a close-hauled course.

(b)   No part of a penalty may be taken inside the *zone* of a rounding *mark* that begins, bounds or ends the leg the boat is on.

(c)   If a boat has one outstanding penalty, she may take the penalty any time after *starting* and before *finishing*. If a boat has two outstanding penalties, she shall take one of them as soon as reasonably possible, but not before *starting*.

(d) When the umpires display a red flag with or soon after a penalty flag, the penalized boat shall take a penalty as soon as reasonably possible, but not before *starting*.

C7.4 Taking and Completing Penalties

(a) When a boat with an outstanding penalty is on a leg to a windward *mark* and gybes, or is on a leg to a leeward *mark* or the finishing line and passes head to wind, she is taking a penalty.

(b) When a boat taking a penalty either does not take the penalty correctly or does not complete the penalty as soon as reasonably possible, she is no longer taking a penalty. The umpires shall signal this as required by rule C5.6.

(c) The umpire boat for each match shall display blue or yellow flags or shapes, each flag or shape indicating one outstanding penalty. When a boat has taken a penalty, or a penalty has been cancelled, one flag or shape shall be removed. Failure of the umpires to display or remove flags or shapes shall not change the number of penalties outstanding.

C8 PENALTIES INITIATED BY UMPIRES

C8.1 Rule Changes

(a) Rules 60.2(a) and 60.3(a) do not apply to *rules* for which penalties may be imposed by umpires.

(b) Rule 64.1(c) is changed so that the provision for exonerating a boat may be applied by the umpires without a hearing, and it takes precedence over any conflicting rule of this appendix.

C8.2

When the umpires decide that a boat has broken rule 31, 42, C4, C7.3(c) or C7.3(d) she shall be penalized by signalling her under rule C5.2 or C5.3. However, if a boat is penalized for breaking a rule of Part 2 and if she in the same incident breaks rule 31, she shall not be penalized for breaking rule 31. Furthermore, a boat that displays an incorrect flag or does not display the correct flag shall be warned orally and given an opportunity to correct the error before being penalized.

C8.3

When the umpires decide that a boat has

(a) gained an advantage by breaking a *rule* after allowing for a penalty,

(b) deliberately broken a *rule*, or

(c) committed a breach of sportsmanship, she shall be penalized under rule C5.2, C5.3 or C5.4.

C8.4 If the umpires or protest committee members decide that a boat may have broken a *rule* other than those listed in rules C6.1(a) and C6.2, they shall so inform the protest committee for its action under rule 60.3 and rule C6.6 when appropriate.

C8.5 When, after one boat has *started*, the umpires are satisfied that the other boat will not *start*, they may signal under rule C5.4 that the boat that did not *start* is disqualified and the match is terminated.

C8.6 When the match umpires, together with at least one other umpire, decide that a boat has broken rule 14 and damage resulted, they may impose a half-point penalty without a hearing. The competitor shall be informed of the penalty as soon as practicable and may request a hearing. The protest committee shall then proceed under rule C6.6. Any penalty decided by the protest committee may be more than half a point. When the umpires decide that a penalty greater than half a point is appropriate, they shall act under rule C8.4.

C9 REQUESTS FOR REDRESS OR REOPENING; APPEALS; OTHER PROCEEDINGS

C9.1 There shall be no request for redress or an appeal from a decision made under rule C5, C6, C7 or C8. In rule 66 the third sentence is changed to 'A *party* to the hearing may not ask for a reopening.'

C9.2 A competitor may not base a request for redress on a claim that an action by an official boat was improper. The protest committee may decide to consider giving redress in such circumstances but only if it believes that an official boat, including an umpire boat, may have seriously interfered with a competing boat.

C9.3 No proceedings of any kind may be taken in relation to any action or non-action by the umpires, except as permitted in rule C9.2.

C10   SCORING

C10.1   The winning competitor of each match scores one point (half a point each for a dead heat); the loser scores no points.

C10.2   When a competitor withdraws from part of an event the scores of all completed races shall stand.

C10.3   When a multiple round robin is terminated with an in-complete round robin, only one point shall be available for all the matches sailed between any two competitors, as follows:

Number of matches completed between any two competitors	*Points for each win*
1	One point
2	Half a point
3	A third of a point
(etc.)	

C10.4   In a round-robin series,
(a)   competitors shall be placed in order of their total scores, highest score first;
(b)   a competitor who has won a match but is disqualified for breaking a *rule* against a competitor in another match shall lose the point for that match (but the losing competitor shall not be awarded the point); and
(c)   the overall position between competitors who have sailed in different groups shall be decided by the highest score.

C10.5   In a knockout series the sailing instructions shall state the minimum number of points required to win a series between two competitors. When a knockout series is terminated it shall be decided in favour of the competitor with the higher score.

C11   TIES

C11.1   Round-Robin Series

In a round-robin series competitors are assigned to one or more groups and scheduled to sail against all other competitors in their group one or more times. Each separate stage identified in the event format shall be a separate round-robin series irrespective of the number of times each competitor sails against each other competitor in that stage.

Ties between two or more competitors in a round-robin series shall be broken by the following methods, in order, until all ties are broken. When one or more ties are only partially broken, rules C11.1(a) to C11.1(e) shall be reapplied to them. Ties shall be decided in favour of the competitor(s) who

(a) placed in order, has the highest score in the matches between the tied competitors;

(b) when the tie is between two competitors in a multiple round robin, has won the last match between the two competitors;

(c) has the most points against the competitor placed highest in the round-robin series or, if necessary, second highest, and so on until the tie is broken. When two separate ties have to be resolved but the resolution of each depends upon resolving the other, the following principles shall be used in the rule C11.1(c) procedure:

   (1) the higher-place tie shall be resolved before the lower- place tie, and

   (2) all the competitors in the lower-place tie shall be treated as a single competitor for the pur-poses of rule C11.1(c);

(d) after applying rule C10.4(c), has the highest place in the different groups, irrespective of the number of competitors in each group;

(e) has the highest place in the most recent stage of the event (fleet race, round robin, etc.).

C11.2 Knockout Series

Ties (including 0–0) between competitors in a knockout series shall be broken by the following methods, in order, until the tie is broken. The tie shall be decided in favour of the competitor who

(a) has the highest place in the most recent round-robin series, applying rule C11.1 if necessary;

(b) has won the most recent match in the event between the tied competitors.

C11.3 Remaining Ties

When rule C11.1 or C11.2 does not resolve a tie,

(a) if the tie needs to be resolved for a later stage of the event (or another event for which the event is a direct qualifier), the tie shall be broken by a sail-off when practicable. When the race committee decides that a sail-off is not practicable, the tie shall be decided in favour of the competitor who has the highest score in the round-robin series after eliminating the score for the first race for each tied competitor or, should this fail to break the tie, the second race for each tied competitor and so on until the tie is broken. When a tie is partially resolved, the remaining tie shall be broken by reapply-ing rule C11.1 or C11.2.

(b) to decide the winner of an event that is not a direct qualifier for another event, or the overall position between competitors eliminated in one round of a knockout series, a sail-off may be used (but not a draw).

(c) when a tie is not broken any monetary prizes or ranking points for tied places shall be added together and divided equally among the tied competitors.

Note: A Standard Notice of Race and Standard Sailing Instructions for match racing are available from the ISAF.

APPENDIX D – TEAM RACING RULES

Team races shall be sailed under The Racing Rules of Sailing *as changed by this appendix. If umpires will be used the sailing instructions shall so state.*

D1   CHANGES TO THE RACING RULES

D1.1   Changes to the Definitions and the Rules of Part 2

(a) In the definition *Zone* the distance is changed to two hull lengths.

(b) The second sentence of rule 18.2(b) is changed to 'If a boat is *clear ahead* when she reaches the *zone*, or she later becomes *clear ahead* when another boat passes head to wind, the boat *clear astern* at that moment shall thereafter give her *Mark-Room*.'

(c) Rule 18.4 is deleted.

(d) Add new rule 23.3: 'A boat that has *finished* shall not act to interfere with a boat that has not *finished*.'

(e) Add new rule 23.4: 'When boats in different races meet, any change of course by either boat shall be consistent with complying with a *rule* or trying to win her own race.'

D1.2 Other Additional Rules

(a) There shall be no penalty for breaking a rule of Part 2 when the incident is between boats on the same team and there is no contact.

(b) Add to rule 41: 'However, a boat may receive help from another boat on her team provided electronic communication is not used.'

(c) A boat is not eligible for redress based on damage or injury caused by another boat on her team.

(d) The first sentence of rule 45 is deleted.

D2 PROTESTS AND PENALTIES

D2.1 Protests and Exoneration

(a) Rule 60.1(a) is changed to 'protest another boat, but not for an alleged breach of a rule of Part 2 unless she was involved in the incident or the incident involved contact between members of the other team; or'.

(b) The third sentence of rule 61.1(a) and all of rule 61.1(a)(2) are deleted.

(c) A boat that, while *racing*, may have broken a rule of Part 2 (except rule 14 when she has caused damage or injury) or rule 42 may take a One-Turn Penalty under rule 44.2.

(d) The sailing instructions may state that rule D2.4(b) applies to all *protests*.

D2.2 Umpired Races

Races to be umpired shall be identified either in the sailing instructions or by the display of flag U no later than the warning signal.

(a) When a boat protests under a rule of Part 2 or under rule 31, 42 or 44, she is not entitled to a hearing. Instead, when the protested boat fails either to acknowledge breaking a *rule* or to take the appropriate penalty, the protesting boat may request a decision by conspicuously displaying a yellow flag and hailing 'Umpire'.

(b) An umpire shall signal a decision as follows:

(1) A green and white flag or a green flag means 'No penalty'.

(2) A red flag means 'One or more boats are penalized.' The umpire shall hail or signal to identify each boat to be penalized.

(c) A boat penalized under rule D2.2(b)(2) shall take a Two-Turns Penalty under rule 44.2.

(d) PENALTIES INITIATED BY UMPIRES
An umpire may take action without a *protest* by another boat when
(1) a boat breaks rule 31 or 42, or a rule of Part 2 through contact with another boat on her team, and does not take a penalty;
(2) a boat fails to comply with rule D2.2(c);
(3) a boat commits a breach of sportsmanship;
(4) a boat breaks rule 14 when damage or injury may have been caused; or
(5) a boat or her team gains an advantage despite taking a penalty.

The umpire may impose a penalty of one or more turns, each including one tack and one gybe, signalled by displaying a red flag and hailing the boat accordingly, or report the incident to the protest committee, signalled by displaying a black flag, or both.

D2.3 Alternative Umpiring Rules
Each of these rules applies only if the sailing instructions so state.
(a) SINGLE-FLAG PROTEST PROCEDURE
Rule D2.2(a) is replaced by
When a boat protests under a rule of Part 2 or under rule 31, 42 or 44, she is not entitled to a hearing. Instead, a boat involved in the incident may promptly acknowledge breaking a *rule* and take the appropriate penalty. If no boat takes a penalty, an umpire shall decide whether any boat has broken a *rule*, and shall signal the decision in compliance with rule D2.2(b).
(b) RACES WITH LIMITED UMPIRING
Rule D2.2 applies, except that when a boat complies with rule D2.2(a) and either there is no decision signalled or an umpire displays a yellow flag signalling he has insufficient facts to decide, the protesting boat is entitled to a hearing.

D2.4 Additional Protest and Redress Rules When Races Are Umpired
(a) Neither the race committee nor the protest committee shall protest a boat for breaking a rule listed in rule D2.2(a). However, upon receipt of a report from any source, the protest committee may protest a boat under rule 14 when damage or injury is alleged.
(b) Protests and requests for redress need not be in writing. The

protest committee may take evidence in any way it considers appropriate and may communicate its decision orally.

(c) There shall be no request for redress or appeal by a boat arising from a decision, action or non-action by an umpire. The protest committee may decide to consider giving redress when it believes that an official boat, including an umpire boat, may have seriously interfered with a competing boat.

D3 SCORING A RACE

D3.1 (a) Each boat *finishing* a race, whether or not rule 28.1 has been complied with, shall be scored points equal to her finishing place. All other boats shall be scored points equal to the number of boats entitled to *race*.

(b) In addition, a boat's points shall be increased as follows:

Rule broken	*Penalty points*
Rule 28.1 when as a result she or her team has gained an advantage	10
Any other *rule* broken while *racing* for which a penalty has not been taken	6

(c) After a hearing the protest committee may penalize as follows:
   (1) When a boat has broken a *rule* and as a result her team has gained an advantage, it may increase that boat's points.
   (2) When a boat has broken rule 1 or 2, rule 14 when she has caused damage or injury, or a *rule* when not *racing*, it may penalize the boat's team by half or more race wins, or it may impose no penalty.

(d) The team with the lower total points wins the race. If the totals are equal, the team that did not have the first-place boat wins.

D3.2 When all boats on one team have *finished*, retired or failed to *start*, the race committee may stop the race. The other team's boats *racing* at that time shall be scored the points they would have received had they *finished*.

D4   SCORING A SERIES

D4.1   When two or more teams are competing in a series, the winner shall be the team scoring the greatest number of race wins. The other teams shall be ranked in order of number of race wins.

D4.2   When necessary, ties in a completed series shall be broken using, in order,

(a)   the number of races won when the tied teams met;
(b)   the points scored when the tied teams met;
(c)   if two teams remain tied, the last race between them;
(d)   total points scored in all races against common opponents;
(e)   a sail-off if possible, otherwise a game of chance.

If a tie is partially resolved by one of these, then the remaining tie shall be broken by starting again at rule D4.2(a).

D4.3   If a series is not completed, teams shall be ranked according to the results from completed rounds, and ties shall be broken whenever possible using the results from races between the tied teams in the incomplete round. If no round has been completed, teams shall be ranked in order of their percentages of races won. Other ties shall be broken as provided in rule D4.2.

D5   BREAKDOWNS WHEN BOATS ARE SUPPLIED BY THE ORGANIZING AUTHORITY

D5.1   A supplied boat suffering a breakdown, and seeking redress as a result, shall display a red flag at the first reasonable opportunity and, if possible, continue *racing*. The race committee shall decide redress as provided in rules D5.2 and D5.3.

D5.2   When the race committee decides that the boat's finishing position was made significantly worse, that the breakdown was through no fault of the crew, and that in the same circumstances a reasonably competent crew would not have been able to avoid the breakdown, it shall make as equitable a decision as possible. This may be to order the race to be resailed or, when the boat's finishing position was predictable, award her points for that position. Any doubt about a boat's position when she broke down shall be resolved against her.

D5.3   A breakdown caused by defective supplied equipment or a breach of a *rule* by an opponent shall not normally be determined to be the fault of the crew, but one caused by careless handling, capsizing or a breach by a boat on the same team shall be. Any doubt about the fault of the crew shall be resolved in the boat's favour.

APPENDIX E – RADIO-CONTROLLED BOAT RACING RULES

Races for radio-controlled boats shall be sailed under The Racing Rules of Sailing *as changed by this appendix.*

E1   TERMINOLOGY, RACE SIGNALS, DEFINITIONS AND FUNDAMENTAL RULES

E1.1   Terminology
'Boat' means a boat that is radio-controlled by a competitor who is not on board. For 'race' used as a noun outside this appendix and outside Appendix A read 'heat'. In this appendix, a race consists of one or more heats and is completed when the last heat in the race is finished. An 'event' consists of one or more races.

E1.2   Race Signals
The section Race Signals is deleted. All signals shall be made orally or by other sounds described in this appendix or the sailing instructions.

E1.3   Definitions
(a)   Add to the definition *Interested Party*: 'but not a competitor when acting as an observer'.
(b)   In the definition *Zone* the distance is changed to four hull lengths.

E1.4   Personal Flotation Devices
Rule 1.2 is changed to 'When on board a rescue boat, each competitor is responsible for wearing a personal flotation device adequate for the conditions.'

E1.5   Aerials
Transmitter aerial extremities shall be adequately protected.

When a protest committee finds that a competitor has broken this rule it shall either warn him and give him time to comply or penalize him.

E2   **PART 2   WHEN BOATS MEET**
Rule 22 is changed to

22   CAPSIZED OR ENTANGLED
If possible, a boat shall avoid a boat that is capsized or entangled, or has not regained control after capsizing or entanglement. A boat is capsized when her masthead is in the water. Two or more boats are entangled when lying together for a period of time so that no boat is capable of manoeuvring to break free of the other(s).

E3   **PART 3   CONDUCT OF A RACE**

E3.1   Races with Observers
The race committee may appoint race observers, who may be competitors. They shall remain in the control area while boats are *racing* and they shall hail and repeat the identity of boats that contact a *mark* or another boat. Such hails shall be made from the control area. Observers shall report all unresolved incidents to the race committee at the end of the heat.

E3.2   Course Board
Rule J2.1(4) is deleted. A course board showing the course and the limits of the control area and launching area(s) shall be located next to or within the control area with information clearly visible to competitors while *racing*.

E3.3   Control and Launching Areas
The control and launching area(s) shall be defined by the sailing instructions. Competitors *racing* shall remain in the control area while a heat is in progress, except that competitors may briefly go to and return from the launching area to perform functions permitted in rule E4.5. Competitors not *racing* shall remain outside the control and launching areas except when offering assistance under rule E4.2 or when acting as race observers.

E3.4   Deleted Rules
The second sentence of rule 25 and all of rule 33 are deleted.

E3.5 Starting Races

Rule 26 is changed to

> Audible signals for starting a heat shall be at one-minute intervals and shall be a warning signal, a preparatory signal and a starting signal. During the minute before the starting signal, oral signals shall be made at ten-second intervals, and during the final ten seconds at one-second intervals. Each signal shall be timed from the beginning of its sound.

E3.6 Starting Penalties

In rules 29.1 and 30 the word 'crew' is deleted. Throughout rule 30 oral announcements shall be used instead of flag signals.

E3.7 Starting and Finishing Lines

The starting and finishing lines shall be tangential to, and on the course side of, the starting and finishing *marks*.

E3.8 Individual Recall

In rule 29.1 replace all after 'the race committee shall promptly' with 'twice hail "Recall (sail numbers)" '.

E3.9 General Recall

In rule 29.2 replace all after 'the race committee may' with 'twice hail "General recall" and make two loud sounds. The warning signal for a new start for the re-called class shall be made shortly thereafter, and the starts for any succeeding classes shall follow the new start.'

E3.10 Shortening or Abandoning after the Start

In rule 32.1(b) 'foul weather' is replaced with 'thunderstorms'. Rule 32.1(c) is deleted.

E4 PART 4 OTHER REQUIREMENTS WHEN RACING

E4.1 Deleted Rules

Rules 43, 47, 48, 49, 50, 52 and 54 are deleted.

E4.2 Outside Help

Rule 41 is changed to

(a) A competitor shall not give tactical or strategic advice to a competitor who is *racing*.

(b) A competitor who is *racing* shall not receive outside help, except

(1) a boat that has gone ashore or aground outside the launching area, or become entangled with another boat or a *mark*, may be freed and relaunched with help from a rescue boat crew;

(2) competitors who are not *racing* and others may give help in the launching area as permitted by rule E4.5;

(3) help in the form of information freely available to all competitors.

E4.3 Propulsion

Rule 42 is changed so that any reference to body movement is deleted. Rule 42.3(f) is also deleted.

E4.4 Penalties for Breaking Rules of Part 2

Throughout rule 44 the penalty shall be the One-Turn Penalty.

E4.5 Launching and Relaunching

Rule 45 is changed to

(a) A boat scheduled to *race* in a heat may be launched, held on the bank, taken ashore or relaunched at any time during the heat. However, she shall not be released between the preparatory and starting signals.

(b) Boats shall be launched or recovered only from within a launching area, except as provided in rule E4.2(b)(1).

(c) While ashore or within a launching area, boats may be adjusted, drained of water or repaired; have their sails changed or reefed; have entangled objects removed; or have radio equipment repaired or changed.

E4.6 Person in Charge

In rule 46 replace 'have on board' with 'be radio-controlled by'.

E4.7 Radio

(a) A competitor shall not transmit radio signals that cause interference with the radio reception of other boats.

(b) A competitor found to have broken rule E4.7(a) shall not *race* until he has proven compliance with that rule.

E4.8 Boat Out of Radio Control

A competitor who loses radio control of his boat shall promptly hail and repeat '(The boat's sail number) out of control'. Such a boat shall be considered to have retired and shall thereafter be an *obstruction*.

E5 **PART 5 PROTESTS, REDRESS, HEARINGS, MISCONDUCT AND APPEALS**

E5.1 **Right to Protest; Right to Request Redress or Rule 69 Action**

Add to rule 60.1(a): 'A *protest* alleging a breach of a rule of Part 2, 3 or 4 shall be made only by a competitor within the control or launching area and by a boat scheduled to *race* in the heat in which the incident occurred.'

E5.2 **Informing the Protestee**

In rule 61.1(a) replace all after the first sentence with 'When her *protest* concerns an incident in the racing area that she is involved in or sees, she shall twice hail "(Her own sail number) protest (the sail number of the other boat)".'

E5.3 **Protest Time Limit**

In rule 61.3 replace 'two hours' with '15 minutes' and add: 'A boat intending to protest shall also inform the race committee no later than five minutes after the end of the relevant heat.'

E5.4 **Accepting Responsibility**

A boat that acknowledges breaking a rule of Part 2, 3 or 4 before the *protest* is found to be valid may retire from the relevant heat without further penalty.

E5.5 **Redress**

(a) Add to rule 62.1:
    (e) radio interference, or
    (f) an entanglement or grounding because of the action of a boat that was breaking a rule of Part 2 or of a vessel not *racing* that was required to keep clear.

(b) In rule 62.2 replace 'two hours' with '15 minutes'.

E5.6 **Right to Be Present**

In rule 63.3(a) replace 'shall have been on board' with 'shall have been radio-controlling them'.

E5.7 **Taking Evidence and Finding Facts**

Add to rule 63.6: 'Evidence about an alleged breach of a rule of Part 2, 3 or 4 given by competitors shall be accepted only from a competitor who was within the control or launching area and whose boat was scheduled to *race* in the heat in which the incident occurred.'

E5.8   Penalties

When a protest committee finds that a boat has broken rule E3.3, E4.2(a) or E4.5, it shall either disqualify her from her next race or require her to make one or more penalty turns in her next race as soon as possible after *starting.*

E5.9   Decisions on Redress

Add to rule 64.2: 'If a boat given redress was damaged, she shall be given reasonable time, but not more than 30 minutes, to effect repairs before her next heat.'

E5.10   Reopening a Hearing

In rule 66 replace '24 hours' with 'ten minutes'.

E6   APPENDIX G   IDENTIFICATION ON SAILS

Appendix G is changed as follows:

(a)   The text of rule G1.1 before rule G1.1(a) is changed to

Every boat of a class administered by ISAF Radio Controlled Sailing shall display a sail number on both sides of each sail. Class insignia and national letters shall be displayed on mainsails as stated in rules G1.1(a), G1.1(b) and E6(f)(1).

(b)   Rule G1.1(c) is changed to

a sail number, which shall be the last two digits of the boat registration number or the competitor's personal number allotted by the relevant issuing authority. A single-digit number shall be prefixed with a '0'. There shall be space in front of a sail number for the prefix '1', which may be required by the race committee where there is a conflict between sail numbers. Where a conflict remains, the race committee shall require that sail numbers be suitably changed until the conflict is resolved. Any prefix '1' or other required change shall become part of the sail number.

(c)   The sentence after rule G1.1(c) is deleted.

(d)   Rule G1.2(b) is changed to

The height of characters and distance between them on the same and opposite sides of the sail shall be as follows:

	Minimum	Maximum
Class insignia:		
Except where positioned back to back, shortest distance between insignia on opposite sides of sail	20mm	
Sail numbers:		
Height of characters	100mm	110mm
Shortest distance between adjoining characters on same side of sail	20mm	30mm
Shortest distance between sail numbers on opposite sides of sail and between sail numbers and other identification	60mm	
National letters:		
Height of characters	60mm	70mm
Shortest distance between adjoining characters on same side of sail	13mm	23mm
Shortest distance between national letters on opposite sides of sail	40mm	

(e) Rule G1.3 is changed to

    (1) Class insignia may be positioned back to back on opposite sides of the sail where the design coincides. Otherwise class insignia, sail numbers and national letters shall be positioned at different heights, with those on the starboard side being uppermost.

    (2) On a mainsail, sail numbers shall be positioned above the national letters and below the class insignia.

    (3) Sail numbers shall be positioned on a mainsail above the line perpendicular to the luff through the quarter leech point.

(f) Where the size of a sail makes it impossible to comply with the minimum dimensions in rule E6(d) or the positioning requirements in rule E6(e)(3), exceptions are permitted in the following order of priority:

    (1) omission of national letters;

    (2) position of the mainsail sail numbers lower than the line perpendicular to the luff through the quarter leech point;

(3) reduction of the shortest distance between sail numbers on opposite sides of the sail provided the shortest distance is not less than 20 mm;

(4) reduction of the height of sail numbers.

APPENDIX F – PROCEDURES FOR APPEALS AND REQUESTS

See rule 70. A national authority may change this appendix by prescription but it shall not be changed by sailing instructions.

F1   APPEALS AND REQUESTS

Appeals, requests by protest committees for confirmation or correction of their decisions, and requests for interpretations of the *rules* shall be made in compliance with this appendix.

F2   SUBMISSION OF DOCUMENTS

F2.1 No later than 15 days after receiving the protest committee's written decision or its decision not to reopen a hearing, the appellant shall send an appeal and a copy of the protest committee's decision to the national authority. The appeal shall state why the appellant believes the protest committee's decision or its procedures were incorrect.

F2.2 The appellant shall also send, with the appeal or as soon as possible thereafter, all of the following documents that are available to her:

(a) the written *protest*(s) or request(s) for redress;

(b) a diagram, prepared or endorsed by the protest committee, showing the positions and tracks of all boats involved, the course to the next *mark* and the required side, the force and direction of the wind, and, if relevant, the depth of water and direction and speed of any current;

(c) the notice of race, the sailing instructions, any other conditions governing the event, and any changes to them;

(d) any additional relevant documents; and

(e) the names, postal and e-mail addresses, and telephone numbers of all *parties* to the hearing and the protest committee chairman.

F2.3 A request from a protest committee for confirmation or correction of its decision shall be sent no later than 15 days after the decision and shall include the decision and the documents listed in rule F2.2. A request for an interpretation of the *rules* shall include assumed facts.

F3 **RESPONSIBILITIES OF NATIONAL AUTHORITY AND PROTEST COMMITTEE**
Upon receipt of an appeal or a request for confirmation or correction, the national authority shall send to the *parties* and protest committee copies of the appeal or request and the protest committee's decision. It shall ask the protest committee for any relevant documents listed in rule F2.2 not sent by the appellant or the protest committee, and the protest committee shall promptly send them to the national authority. When the national authority has received them it shall send copies to the *parties*.

F4 **COMMENTS**
The *parties* and protest committee may make comments on the appeal or request or on any of the documents listed in rule F2.2 by sending them in writing to the national authority. Comments on any document shall be made no later than 15 days after receiving it from the national authority. The national authority shall send copies of the comments to the *parties* and protest committee as appropriate.

F5 **INADEQUATE FACTS; REOPENING**
The national authority shall accept the protest committee's finding of facts except when it decides they are inadequate. In that case it shall require the committee to provide additional facts or other information, or to reopen the hearing and report any new finding of facts, and the committee shall promptly do so.

F6 **WITHDRAWING AN APPEAL**
An appellant may withdraw an appeal before it is decided by accepting the protest committee's decision.

APPENDIX G – IDENTIFICATION ON SAILS

See rule 77.

G1   ISAF INTERNATIONAL CLASS BOATS

G1.1   Identification

Every boat of an ISAF International Class or Recognized Class shall carry on her mainsail and, as provided in rules G1.3(d) and G1.3(e) for letters and numbers only, on her spinnaker and headsail

(a)   the insignia denoting her class;

(b)   at all international events, except when the boats are provided to all competitors, national letters denoting her national authority from the table below. For the purposes of this rule, international events are ISAF events, world and continental championships, and events described as international events in their notices of race and sailing instructions; and

(c)   a sail number of no more than four digits allotted by her national authority or, when so required by the class rules, by the international class association. The four-digit limitation does not apply to classes whose ISAF membership or recognition took effect before 1 April 1997. Alternatively, if permitted in the class rules, an owner may be allotted a personal sail number by the relevant issuing authority, which may be used on all his boats in that class.

Sails measured before 31 March 1999 shall comply with rule G1.1 or with the rules applicable at the time of measurement.

NATIONAL SAIL LETTERS

National authority	Letters	National authority	Letters
Algeria	ALG	Antigua	ANT
American Samoa	ASA	Argentina	ARG
Andorra	AND	Armenia	ARM
Angola	ANG	Australia	AUS

National authority	Letters	National authority	Letters
Austria	AUT	Ireland	IRL
Azerbaijan	AZE	Israel	ISR
Bahamas	BAH	Italy	ITA
Bahrain	BRN	Jamaica	JAM
Barbados	BAR	Japan	JPN
Belarus	BLR	Kazakhstan	KAZ
Belgium	BEL	Kenya	KEN
Bermuda	BER	Korea	KOR
Brazil	BRA	Kuwait	KUW
British Virgin Islands	IVB	Kyrgyzstan	KGZ
Bulgaria	BUL	Latvia	LAT
Canada	CAN	Lebanon	LIB
Cayman Islands	CAY	Libya	LBA
Chile	CHI	Liechtenstein	LIE
China, PR	CHN	Lithuania	LTU
Chinese Taipei	TPE	Luxembourg	LUX
Colombia	COL	Macedonia (FYRO)	MKD
Cook Islands	COK	Malaysia	MAS
Croatia	CRO	Malta	MLT
Cuba	CUB	Mauritius	MRI
Cyprus	CYP	Mexico	MEX
Czech Republic	CZE	Micronesia (FSo)	FSM
Denmark	DEN	Moldova	MDA
Dominican Republic	DOM	Monaco	MON
Ecuador	ECU	Montenegro	MNE
Egypt	EGY	Morocco	MAR
El Salvador	ESA	Myanmar	MYA
Estonia	EST	Namibia	NAM
Fiji	FIJ	Netherlands	NED
Finland	FIN	Netherlands Antilles	AHO
France	FRA	New Zealand	NZL
Georgia	GEO	Norway	NOR
Germany	GER	Oman	OMA
Great Britain	GBR	Pakistan	PAK
Greece	GRE	Palestine	PLE
Grenada	GRN	Papua New Guinea	PNG
Guam	GUM	Paraguay	PAR
Guatemala	GUA	Peru	PER
Hong Kong	HKG	Philippines	PHI
Hungary	HUN	Poland	POL
Iceland	ISL	Portugal	POR
India	IND	Puerto Rico	PUR
Indonesia	INA	Qatar	QAT

National authority	Letters	National authority	Letters
Romania	ROU	Sweden	SWE
Russia	RUS	Switzerland	SUI
Samoa	SAM	Tahiti	TAH
San Marino	SMR	Thailand	THA
Senegal	SEN	Trinidad & Tobago	TRI
Serbia	SRB	Tunisia	TUN
Seychelles	SEY	Turkey	TUR
Singapore	SIN	Ukraine	UKR
Slovak Republic	SVK	United Arab Emirates	UAE
Slovenia	SLO	United States of America	USA
Solomon Islands	SOL	Uruguay	URU
South Africa	RSA	US Virgin Islands	ISV
Spain	ESP	Vanuatu	VAN
Sri Lanka	SRI	Venezuela	VEN
St Lucia	LCA	Zimbabwe	ZIM

Note: An up-to-date list is available on the ISAF website.

G1.2 Specifications

(a) National letters and sail numbers shall be in capital letters and Arabic numerals, clearly legible and of the same colour. Commercially available typefaces giving the same or better legibility than Helvetica are acceptable.

(b) The height of characters and space between adjoining characters on the same and opposite sides of the sail shall be related to the boat's overall length as follows:

Overall length	Minimum height	Minimum space between characters and from edge of sail
under 3.5 m	230 mm	45 mm
3.5 m–8.5 m	300 mm	60 mm
8.5 m–11 m	375 mm	75 mm
over 11 m	450 mm	90 mm

G1.3 Positioning

Class insignia, national letters and sail numbers shall be positioned as follows:

(a) Except as provided in rules G1.3(d) and G1.3(e), class insignia, national letters and sail numbers shall when possible be wholly above an arc whose centre is the head point and whose radius is 60% of the leech length. They shall be placed at different heights on the two sides of the sail, those on the starboard side being uppermost.

(b) The class insignia shall be placed above the national letters. If the class insignia is of such a design that two of them coincide when placed back to back on both sides of the sail, they may be so placed.

(c) National letters shall be placed above the sail number.

(d) The national letters and sail number shall be displayed on the front side of a spinnaker but may be placed on both sides. They shall be displayed wholly below an arc whose centre is the head point and whose radius is 40% of the foot median and, when possible, wholly above an arc whose radius is 60% of the foot median.

(e) The national letters and sail number shall be displayed on both sides of a headsail whose clew can extend behind the mast 30% or more of the mainsail foot length. They shall be displayed wholly below an arc whose centre is the head point and whose radius is half the luff length and, if possible, wholly above an arc whose radius is 75% of the luff length.

G2 OTHER BOATS

Other boats shall comply with the rules of their national authority or class association in regard to the allotment, carrying and size of insignia, letters and numbers. Such rules shall, when practicable, conform to the above requirements.

G3 CHARTERED OR LOANED BOATS

When so stated in the notice of race or sailing instructions, a boat chartered or loaned for an event may carry national letters or a sail number in contravention of her class rules.

G4 WARNINGS AND PENALTIES

When a protest committee finds that a boat has broken a rule of this appendix it shall either warn her and give her time to comply or penalize her.

G5 CHANGES BY CLASS RULES

ISAF classes may change the rules of this appendix provided the changes have first been approved by the ISAF.

APPENDIX H – WEIGHING CLOTHING AND EQUIPMENT

See rule 43. This appendix shall not be changed by sailing instructions or prescriptions of national authorities.

H1   Items of clothing and equipment to be weighed shall be arranged on a rack. After being saturated in water the items shall be allowed to drain freely for one minute before being weighed. The rack must allow the items to hang as they would hang from clothes hangers, so as to allow the water to drain freely. Pockets that have drain-holes that cannot be closed shall be empty, but pockets or items that can hold water shall be full.

H2   When the weight recorded exceeds the amount permitted, the competitor may rearrange the items on the rack and the equipment inspector or measurer shall again soak and weigh them. This procedure may be repeated a second time if the weight still exceeds the amount permitted.

H3   A competitor wearing a dry suit may choose an alternative means of weighing the items.
(a)   The dry suit and items of clothing and equipment that are worn outside the dry suit shall be weighed as described above.
(b)   Clothing worn underneath the dry suit shall be weighed as worn while *racing*, without draining.
(c)   The two weights shall be added together.

APPENDIX J – NOTICE OF RACE AND SAILING INSTRUCTIONS

See rules 89.2(a) and 90.2. The term 'race' includes a regatta or other series of races.

J1   **NOTICE OF RACE CONTENTS**

J1.1   The notice of race shall include the following information:
(1)   the title, place and dates of the race and name of the organizing authority;

(2) that the race will be governed by the *rules* as defined in *The Racing Rules of Sailing*;

(3) a list of any other documents that will govern the event (for example, *The Equipment Rules of Sailing*, to the extent that they apply), stating where or how each document or a copy of it may be seen;

(4) the classes to race, any handicap or rating system that will be used and the classes to which it will apply, conditions of entry and any restrictions on entries;

(5) the times of registration and warning signals for the practice race, if one is scheduled, and the first race, and succeeding races if known.

J1.2 The notice of race shall include any of the following that will apply and that would help competitors decide whether to attend the event or that conveys other information they will need before the sailing instructions become available:

(1) identification of any racing rules that will be changed, a summary of the changes, and a statement that the changes will appear in full in the sailing instructions (see rule 86);

(2) that advertising will be restricted to Category A or that boats will be required to display advertising chosen and supplied by the organizing authority (see ISAF Regulation 20) and other information related to Regulation 20;

(3) any classification requirements that some or all competitors must satisfy (see rule 79 and ISAF Regulation 22, Sailor Classification Code);

(4) for an event where entries from other countries are expected, any national prescriptions that may require advance preparation;

(5) the procedure for advance registration or entry, including fees and any closing dates;

(6) an entry form, to be signed by the boat's owner or owner's representative, containing words such as 'I agree to be bound by *The Racing Rules of Sailing* and by all other *rules* that govern this event.';

(7) equipment inspection, measurement procedures or requirements for measurement certificates or for handicap or rating certificates;

(8) the time and place at which the sailing instructions will be available;

(9) changes to class rules, as permitted under rule 87, referring specifically to each rule and stating the change;

(10) the courses to be sailed;

(11) the penalty for breaking a rule of Part 2, other than the Two-Turns Penalty;

(12) denial of the right of appeal, subject to rule 70.5;

(13) the scoring system, if different from the Low Point System in Appendix A, the number of races scheduled and the minimum number that must be completed to constitute a series;

(14) prizes.

J2 SAILING INSTRUCTION CONTENTS

J2.1 The sailing instructions shall include the following information:

(1) that the race will be governed by the *rules* as defined in *The Racing Rules of Sailing*;

(2) a list of any other documents that will govern the event (for example, *The Equipment Rules of Sailing*, to the extent that they apply);

(3) the schedule of races, the classes to race and times of warning signals for each class;

(4) the course(s) to be sailed, or a list of *marks* from which the course will be selected and, if relevant, how courses will be signalled;

(5) descriptions of *marks*, including starting and finishing *marks*, stating the order and side on which each is to be left and identifying all rounding *marks* (see rule 28.1);

(6) descriptions of the starting and finishing lines, class flags and any special signals to be used;

(7) the time limit, if any, for *finishing*;

(8) the handicap or rating system to be used, if any, and the classes to which it will apply;

(9) the scoring system, if different from the Low Point System in Appendix A, included by reference to Appendix A, to class rules or other *rules* governing the event, or stated in full. State the number of races scheduled and the minimum number that must be completed to constitute a series.

J2.2 The sailing instructions shall include those of the following that will apply:

(1) that advertising will be restricted to Category A (see ISAF Regulation 20) and other information related to Regulation 20;

(2) replacement of the rules of Part 2 with the right-of-way rules of the *International Regulations for Preventing Collisions at Sea* or other government right-of-way rules, the time(s) or place(s) they will apply, and any night signals to be used by the race committee;

(3) changes to the racing rules permitted by rule 86, referring specifically to each rule and stating the change (if rule 86.2 applies, state the authorization);

(4) changes to the national prescriptions (see rule 88);

(5) when appropriate, at an event where entries from other countries are expected, a copy in English of the national prescriptions that will apply;

(6) changes to class rules, as permitted under rule 87, referring specifically to each rule and stating the change;

(7) restrictions controlling changes to boats when supplied by the organizing authority;

(8) the registration procedure;

(9) measurement or inspection procedure;

(10) location(s) of official notice board(s);

(11) procedure for changing the sailing instructions;

(12) safety requirements, such as requirements and signals for personal flotation devices, check-in at the starting area, and check-out and check-in ashore;

(13) declaration requirements;

(14) signals to be made ashore and location of signal station(s);

(15) the racing area (a chart is recommended);

(16) approximate course length and approximate length of windward legs;

(17) description of any area designated by the race committee to be an *obstruction* (see the definition *Obstruction*);

(18) the time limit, if any, for the first boat to *finish* and the time limit, if any, for boats other than the first boat to *finish*;

(19) time allowances;

(20) the location of the starting area and any restrictions on entering it;

(21) any special procedures or signals for individual or general recall;

(22) boats identifying *mark* locations;

(23) any special procedures or signals for changing a leg of the course (see rule 33);

(24) any special procedures for shortening the course or for *finishing* a shortened course;

(25) restrictions on use of support boats, plastic pools, radios, etc.; on trash disposal; on hauling out; and on outside assistance provided to a boat that is not *racing*;

(26) the penalty for breaking a rule of Part 2, other than the Two-Turns Penalty;

(27) under rule 86.1(b), a change to the number of hull lengths determining the *zone*;

(28) whether rule 67 or Appendix P will apply;

(29) protest procedure and times and place of hearings;

(30) if rule N1.4(b) will apply, the time limit for requesting a hearing under that rule;

(31) when required by rule 70.3, the national authority to which appeals and requests may be sent and, when applicable, subject to rule 70.5 denial of the right of appeal;

(32) the national authority's approval of the appointment of an international jury, when required under rule 91(b);

(33) substitution of competitors;

(34) the minimum number of boats appearing in the starting area required for a race to be started;

(35) when and where races *postponed* or *abandoned* for the day will be resailed;

(36) tides and currents;

(37) prizes;

(38) other commitments of the race committee and obligations of boats.

APPENDIX K – NOTICE OF RACE GUIDE

This guide provides a notice of race designed primarily for major championship regattas for one or more classes. It therefore will be particularly useful for world, continental and national championships and other events of similar importance. It can be downloaded from the ISAF website (www.sailing.org) as a basic text for producing a notice of race for any particular event.

The guide can also be useful for other events. However, for such events some of the paragraphs will be unnecessary or undesirable. Organizing authorities should therefore be careful in making their choices.

This guide relates closely to Appendix L, Sailing Instructions Guide, and its expanded version Appendix LE on the ISAF website, the introduction to which contains principles that also apply to a notice of race.

To use this guide, first review rule J1 and decide which paragraphs will be needed. Paragraphs that are required by rule J1.1 are marked with an asterisk (*). Delete all inapplicable or unnecessary paragraphs. Select the version preferred where there is a choice. Follow the directions in the left margin to fill in the spaces where a solid line (_____) appears and select the preferred wording if a choice or option is shown in brackets ([. . .]).

After deleting unused paragraphs, renumber all paragraphs in sequential order. Be sure that paragraph numbers are correct where one paragraph refers to another.

The items listed below, when applicable, should be distributed with the notice of race, but should not be included as numbered paragraphs in the notice.

1   *An entry form, to be signed by the boat's owner or owner's representative, containing words such as 'I agree to be bound by* The Racing Rules of Sailing *and by all other rules that govern this event.'*

2   *For an event where entries from other countries are expected, the applicable national prescriptions in English.*

3   *List of sponsors, if appropriate.*

4   *Lodging and camping information.*

5   *Description of meal facilities.*

6   *Race committee and protest committee members.*

7   *Special mooring or storage requirements.*

8   *Sail and boat repair facilities and ship's chandlers.*

9   *Charter boat availability.*

On separate lines, insert the full name of the regatta, the inclusive dates from measurement or the practice race until the final race or closing ceremony, the name of the organizing authority, and the city and country.

_____

_____

_____

_____

NOTICE OF RACE

1   RULES

1.1*   The regatta will be governed by the rules as defined in *The Racing Rules of Sailing*.

Use the first sentence if appropriate. Insert the name. List by number and title the prescriptions that will not apply (see rule 88). Use the second sentence if it applies and if entries from other countries are expected, and state the relevant prescriptions in full.

1.2   [The following prescriptions of the _____ national authority will not apply: _____.] [The prescriptions that may require advance preparation are stated in full below.]

(OR)

Use only if the national authority for the venue of the event has not adopted a prescription to rule 88.

1.2   No national prescriptions will apply.

List by name any other documents that govern the event; for example, The Equipment Rules of Sailing, to the extent that they apply.

1.3*   _____ will apply.

See rule 86. Insert the rule number(s) and summarize the changes.

1.4   Racing rule(s) _____ will be changed as follows: _____. The changes will appear in full in the sailing instructions. The sailing instructions may also change other racing rules.

Insert the rule number(s) and class name. Make a separate statement for the rules of each class.

1.5   Under rule 87, rule(s) _____ of the _____ class rules [will not apply] [is (are) changed as follows: _____].

1.6   If there is a conflict between languages the English text will take precedence.

2 ADVERTISING

See ISAF Regulation 20. Include other applicable information related to Regulation 20.

2.1 Advertising will be restricted to Category A.

See ISAF Regulation 20.3(d).

2.2 Boats may be required to display advertising chosen and supplied by the organizing authority.

3* ELIGIBILITY AND ENTRY

Insert the class(es).

3.1 The regatta is open to all boats of the _____ class(es).

(OR)

Insert the class(es) and eligibility requirements.

3.1 The regatta is open to boats of the _____ class(es) that _____.

Insert the postal, fax and e-mail addresses and entry closing date.

3.2 Eligible boats may enter by completing the attached form and sending it, together with the required fee, to _____ by _____.

Insert any conditions.

3.3 Late entries will be accepted under the following conditions: _____.

Insert any restrictions.

3.4 The following restrictions on the number of boats apply: _____.

Insert any requirements.

4 CLASSIFICATION

The following classification requirements will apply (see rule 79): _____.

5 FEES

Insert all required fees for racing.

5.1 Required fees are as follows:

Class	Fee
_____	_____
_____	_____
_____	_____

<table>
<tr><td>

Insert optional fees (eg for social events).

</td><td>

5.2

</td><td>

Other fees:

_____

_____

</td></tr>
<tr><td>

Use only when a class is divided into fleets racing a qualifying series and a final series.

</td><td>

6

</td><td>

QUALIFYING SERIES AND FINAL SERIES

The regatta will consist of a qualifying series and a final series.

</td></tr>
<tr><td></td><td>

7

</td><td>

SCHEDULE

</td></tr>
<tr><td>

Insert the day, date and times.

</td><td>

7.1*

</td><td>

Registration:

Day and date _____

From _____   To _____

</td></tr>
<tr><td>

Insert the day, date and times.

</td><td>

7.2

</td><td>

Measurement and inspection:

Day and date _____

From _____   To _____

</td></tr>
</table>

<table>
<tr><td>

Revise as desired and insert the dates and classes. Include a practice race if any. When the series consists of qualifying races and final races, specify them. The schedule can also be given in an attachment.

</td><td>

7.3*

</td><td>

Dates of racing:

</td></tr>
</table>

Date	Class _____	Class _____
_____	racing	racing
_____	racing	reserve day
_____	reserve day	racing
_____	racing	racing
_____	racing	racing

<table>
<tr><td>

Insert the classes and numbers.

</td><td>

7.4

</td><td>

Number of races:

</td></tr>
</table>

Class	Number	Races per day
_____	_____	_____
_____	_____	_____

<table>
<tr><td>

Insert the time.

</td><td>

7.5*

</td><td>

The scheduled time of the warning signal for the [practice race] [first race] [each day] is _____.

</td></tr>
</table>

8 MEASUREMENTS
Each boat shall produce a valid [measurement] [rating] certificate.

(OR)

List the measurements with appropriate references to the class rules.

Each boat shall produce a valid [measurement] [rating] certificate. In addition the following measurements [may] [will] be taken: _____.

Insert the time, date and location.

9 SAILING INSTRUCTIONS
The sailing instructions will be available after _____ on _____ at _____.

10 VENUE

Insert a number or letter. Provide a marked map with driving instructions.

10.1 Attachment _____ shows the location of the regatta harbour.

Insert a number or letter. Provide a marked map or chart.

10.2 Attachment _____ shows the location of the racing areas.

Include the description.

11 THE COURSES
The courses to be sailed will be as follows: _____.

(OR)

Insert a number or letter. A method of illustrating various courses is shown in Addendum A of Appendix L or LE. Insert the course length if applicable.

The diagrams in Attachment _____ show the courses, including the approximate angles between legs, the order in which marks are to be passed, and the side on which each mark is to be left. [The approximate course length will be _____.]

12 PENALTY SYSTEM

Include paragraph 12.1 only when the Two-Turns Penalty will not be used. Insert the number of places or describe the penalties.

12.1 The Scoring Penalty, rule 44.3, will apply. The penalty will be _____ places.

(OR)

12.1 The penalties are as follows: _____.

Insert the class(es).   **12.2** For the _____ class(es) rule 44.1 is changed so that the Two-Turns Penalty is replaced by the One-Turn Penalty.

Include only if the protest committee is an international jury or another provision of rule 70.5 applies. Use 'jury' only if referring to an international jury.   **12.3** Decisions of the [protest committee] [jury] will be final as provided in rule 70.5.

13   SCORING

Include only if the Low Point System is replaced by the Bonus Point System.   **13.1** The Bonus Point System of Appendix A will apply.

(OR)

Include only if neither of the Appendix A scoring systems will be used. Describe the system.   **13.1** The scoring system is as follows: _____.

Insert the number.   **13.2** _____ races are required to be completed to constitute a series.

Insert the numbers throughout.   **13.3** (a) When fewer than _____ races have been completed, a boat's series score will be the total of her race scores.

  (b) When from _____ to _____ races have been completed, a boat's series score will be the total of her race scores excluding her worst score.

  (c) When _____ or more races have been completed, a boat's series score will be the total of her race scores excluding her two worst scores.

Insert the identification markings. National letters are suggested for international events.   **14   SUPPORT BOATS**
Support boats shall be marked with _____.

15   BERTHING

Boats shall be kept in their assigned places in the [boat park] [harbour].

16   HAUL-OUT RESTRICTIONS

Keelboats shall not be hauled out during the regatta except with and according to the terms of prior written permission of the race committee.

17   DIVING EQUIPMENT AND PLASTIC POOLS

Underwater breathing apparatus and plastic pools or their equivalent shall not be used around keelboats between the preparatory signal of the first race and the end of the regatta.

Insert any alternative text that applies. Describe the radio communication bands or frequencies that will be used or allowed.

18   RADIO COMMUNICATION

Except in an emergency, a boat shall neither make radio transmissions while racing nor receive radio communications not available to all boats. This restriction also applies to mobile telephones.

If perpetual trophies will be awarded state their complete names.

19   PRIZES

Prizes will be given as follows: _____.

The laws applicable to the venue in which the event is held may limit disclaimers. Any disclaimer should be drafted to comply with those laws.

20   DISCLAIMER OF LIABILITY

Competitors participate in the regatta entirely at their own risk. See rule 4, Decision to Race. The organizing authority will not accept any liability for material damage or personal injury or death sustained in conjunction with or prior to, during, or after the regatta.

Insert the currency and amount.

21   INSURANCE

Each participating boat shall be insured with valid third-party liability insurance with a minimum cover of _____ per event or the equivalent.

Insert necessary contact information

22   FURTHER INFORMATION

For further information please contact _____.

APPENDIX L – SAILING INSTRUCTIONS GUIDE

This guide provides a set of tested sailing instructions designed primarily for major championship regattas for one or more classes. It therefore will be particularly useful for world, continental and national championships and other events of similar importance. The guide can also be useful for other events; however, for such events some of these instructions will be unnecessary or undesirable. Race officers should therefore be careful in making their choices.

An expanded version of the guide, Appendix LE, is available on the ISAF website (www.sailing.org). It contains provisions applicable to the largest and most complicated multi-class events, as well as variations on several of the sailing instructions recommended in this appendix. It will be revised from time to time, to reflect advances in race management techniques as they develop, and can be downloaded as a basic text for producing the sailing instructions for any particular event. Appendix L can also be downloaded from the ISAF website.

The principles on which all sailing instructions should be based are as follows:

1   *They should include only two types of statement: the intentions of the race committee and protest committee and the obligations of competitors.*
2   *They should be concerned only with racing. Information about social events, assignment of moorings, etc., should be provided separately.*
3   *They should not change the racing rules except when clearly desirable. (When they do so, they must follow rule 86 by referring specifically to the rule being changed and stating the change.)*
4   *They should not repeat or restate any of the racing rules.*
5   *They should not repeat themselves.*
6   *They should be in chronological order; that is, the order in which the competitor will use them.*
7   *They should, when possible, use words or phrases from the racing rules.*

To use this guide, first review rule J2 and decide which instructions will be needed. Instructions that are required by rule J2.1 are *marked with an asterisk (*). Delete all inapplicable or unnecessary instructions. Select the version preferred where there is a choice. Follow the directions in the left margin to fill in the spaces where a solid line (_____) appears and select the preferred wording if a choice or option is shown in brackets ([. . .]).*

After deleting unused instructions, renumber all instructions in sequential order. Be sure that instruction numbers are correct where one instruction refers to another.

On separate lines, insert the full name of the regatta, the inclusive dates from measurement or the practice race until the final race or closing ceremony, the name of the organizing authority, and the city and country.

_____

_____

_____

_____

SAILING INSTRUCTIONS

1 RULES

1.1* The regatta will be governed by the rules as defined in *The Racing Rules of Sailing*.

Use the first sentence if appropriate. Insert the name. List by number and title the prescriptions that will not apply (see rule 88). Use the second sentence if it applies and if entries from other national authorities are expected, and state the prescriptions in full.

1.2 [The following prescriptions of the _____ national authority will not apply: _____.] [The prescriptions that will apply are stated in full below.]

(OR)

Use only if the national authority for the venue of the event has not adopted a prescription to rule 88.

1.2 No national prescriptions will apply.

1.3* _____ will apply.

1.4 Racing rule(s) _____ will be changed as follows: _____.

1.5 Under rule 86.1(b), in the definition Zone the
distance is changed to [two] [four] hull
lengths.

1.6 Under rule 87, rule(s) _____ of the _____ class
rules [will not apply] [is (are) changed as fol-
lows: _____].

1.7 If there is a conflict between languages the
English text will take precedence.

2 **NOTICES TO COMPETITORS**
Notices to competitors will be posted on the
official notice board(s) located at _____.

3 **CHANGES TO SAILING INSTRUCTIONS**
Any change to the sailing instructions will be
posted before 0900 on the day it will take
effect, except that any change to the schedule
of races will be posted by 2000 on the day
before it will take effect.

4 **SIGNALS MADE ASHORE**

4.1 Signals made ashore will be displayed at
_____.

Insert the number of minutes.

4.2   When flag AP is displayed ashore, '1 minute' is replaced with 'not less than _____ minutes' in the race signal AP.

(OR)

Insert the number of minutes.

4.2   Flag D with one sound means 'The warning signal will be made not less than _____ minutes after flag D is displayed. [Boats are requested not to leave the harbour until this signal is made.]'

Delete if covered by a class rule.

4.3   When flag Y is displayed ashore, rule 40 applies at all times while afloat. This changes the Part 4 preamble.

5   SCHEDULE OF RACES

Revise as desired and insert the dates and classes. Include a practice race if any. When the series consists of qualifying races and final races, specify them. The schedule can also be given in an attachment.

Insert the classes and numbers.

5.1*   Dates of racing:

Date	Class _____	Class _____
_____	racing	racing
_____	racing	reserve day
_____	reserve day	racing
_____	racing	racing
_____	racing	racing

5.2*   Number of races:

Class	Number	Races per day
_____	_____	_____
_____	_____	_____

One extra race per day may be sailed, provided that no class becomes more than one race ahead of schedule and the change is made according to instruction 3.

Insert the time.

5.3*   The scheduled time of the warning signal for the first race each day is _____.

5.4 After a long postponement, to alert boats that a race or sequence of races will begin soon, an orange flag will be displayed with one sound for at least four minutes before a warning signal is displayed.

Insert the time. **5.5** On the last day of the regatta no warning signal will be made after _____.

Insert the classes and names or descriptions of the flags. **6*** **CLASS FLAGS**
Class flags will be:

Class	Flag
_____	_____
_____	_____
_____	_____

Insert a number or letter. **7** **RACING AREAS**
Attachment _____ shows the location of racing areas.

8 **THE COURSES**

Insert a number or letter. A method of illustrating various courses is shown in Addendum A. Insert the course length if applicable. **8.1*** The diagrams in Attachment _____ show the courses, including the approximate angles between legs, the order in which marks are to be passed, and the side on which each mark is to be left. [The approximate course length will be _____.]

8.2 No later than the warning signal, the race committee signal boat will display the approximate compass bearing of the first leg.

8.3 Courses will not be shortened. This changes rule 32.

Include only when changing positions of marks is impracticable. **8.4** Legs of the course will not be changed after the preparatory signal. This changes rule 33.

9 MARKS

Change the mark numbers as needed and insert the descriptions of the marks. Use the second alternative when Marks 4S and 4P form a gate, with Mark 4S to be left to starboard and Mark 4P to port.

Change the mark numbers as needed and insert the descriptions of the marks. Use the second alternative when Marks 4S and 4P form a gate, with Mark 4S to be left to starboard and Mark 4P to port.

9.1* Marks 1, 2, 3 and 4 will be _____.

(OR)

9.1* Marks 1, 2, 3, 4S and 4P will be _____.

Unless clear from the course diagrams, list the marks that are rounding marks.

9.2 The following marks are rounding marks: _____.

Insert the descriptions of the marks.

9.3 New marks, as provided in instruction 12.1, will be _____.

Describe the starting and finishing marks: for example, the race committee signal boat at the starboard end and a buoy at the port end. Instruction 11.2 will describe the starting line and instruction 13 the finishing line.

9.4* The starting and finishing marks will be _____.

9.5 A race committee boat signalling a change of a leg of the course is a mark as provided in instruction 12.2.

Describe each area by its location and any easily recognized details of appearance.

10 AREAS THAT ARE OBSTRUCTIONS

The following areas are designated as obstructions: _____.

11 THE START

Include only if the asterisked option in rule 26 will be used. Insert the number of minutes.

11.1 Races will be started by using rule 26 with the warning signal made _____ minutes before the starting signal.

(OR)

Describe any starting system other than that stated in rule 26.

11.1 Races will be started as follows: _____. This changes rule 26.

11.2*The starting line will be between staffs displaying orange flags on the starting marks.

(OR)

11.2*The starting line will be between a staff displaying an orange flag on the starting mark at the starboard end and the port-end starting mark.

(OR)

Insert the description.

11.2*The starting line will be _____.

11.3 Boats whose warning signal has not been made shall avoid the starting area during the starting sequence for other races.

Insert the number of minutes.

11.4 A boat starting later than _____ minutes after her starting signal will be scored Did Not Start without a hearing. This changes rule A4.

Insert the channel number.

11.5 If any part of a boat's hull, crew or equipment is on the course side of the starting line during the two minutes before her starting signal and she is identified, the race committee will attempt to broadcast her sail number on VHF channel _____. Failure to make a broadcast or to time it accurately will not be grounds for a request for redress. This changes rule 62.1(a).

12   CHANGE OF THE NEXT LEG OF THE COURSE

12.1 To change the next leg of the course, the race committee will move the original mark (or the finishing line) to a new position.

(OR)

12.1 To change the next leg of the course, the race committee will lay a new mark (or move the finishing line) and remove the original mark as soon as practicable. When in a subsequent change a new mark is replaced, it will be replaced by an original mark.

Reverse 'port' and 'starboard' when the mark is to be left to starboard.

12.2 Except at a gate, boats shall pass between the race committee boat signalling the change of the next leg and the nearby mark, leaving the mark to port and the race committee boat to starboard. This changes rule 28.1.

13* **THE FINISH**

The finishing line will be between staffs displaying orange flags on the finishing marks.

(OR)

The finishing line will be between a staff displaying an orange flag on the finishing mark at the starboard end and the port-end finishing mark.

(OR)

Insert the description.

The finishing line will be _____.

14 **PENALTY SYSTEM**

Include instruction 14.1 only when the Two-Turns Penalty will not be used.

14.1 The Scoring Penalty, rule 44.3, will apply. The penalty will be _____ places.

(OR)

Insert the number of places or describe the penalties.

14.1 The penalties are as follows: _____.

Insert the class(es).

14.2 For the _____ class(es) rule 44.1 is changed so that the Two-Turns Penalty is replaced by the One-Turn Penalty.

Here and below, use 'jury' only when referring to an international jury.

14.3 As provided in rule 67, the [protest committee] [jury] may, without a hearing, penalize a boat that has broken rule 42.

(OR)

Unless all of Appendix P applies, state any restrictions.

14.3 Appendix P will apply [as changed by instruction(s) [14.2] [and] [14.4]].

Recommended only for junior events.

14.4 Rule P2.3 will not apply and rule P2.2 is changed so that it will apply to any penalty after the first one.

15 TIME LIMITS AND TARGET TIMES

Insert the classes and times. Omit the Mark 1 time limit if inapplicable.

15.1* Time limits and target times are as follows:

Class	Time limit	Mark 1 time limit	Target time
_____	_____	_____	_____
_____	_____	_____	_____
_____	_____	_____	_____

If no boat has passed Mark 1 within the Mark 1 time limit the race will be abandoned. Failure to meet the target time will not be grounds for redress. This changes rule 62.1(a).

Insert the time (or different times for different classes).

15.2 Boats failing to finish within _____ after the first boat sails the course and finishes will be scored Did Not Finish without a hearing. This changes rules 35, A4 and A5.

16 PROTESTS AND REQUESTS FOR REDRESS

State the location if necessary.

16.1 Protest forms are available at the race office[, located at _____]. Protests and requests for redress or reopening shall be delivered there within the appropriate time limit.

Change the time if different.

16.2 For each class, the protest time limit is 90 minutes after the last boat has finished the last race of the day.

Change the posting time if different. Insert the protest room location and, if applicable, the time for the first hearing.

16.3 Notices will be posted no later than 30 minutes after the protest time limit to inform competitors of hearings in which they are parties or named as witnesses. Hearings will be held in the protest room, located at _____, beginning at [the time posted] [_____].

16.4 Notices of protests by the race committee or [protest committee] [jury] will be posted to inform boats under rule 61.1(b).

16.5 A list of boats that, under instruction 14.3, have been penalized for breaking rule 42 will be posted.

16.6 Breaches of instructions 11.3, 18, 21, 23, 24, 25, 26 and 27 will not be grounds for a protest by a boat. This changes rule 60.1(a). Penalties for these breaches may be less than disqualification if the [protest committee] [jury] so decides. The scoring abbreviation for a discretionary penalty imposed under this instruction will be DPI.

16.7 On the last scheduled day of racing a request for reopening a hearing shall be delivered
   (a) within the protest time limit if the requesting party was informed of the decision on the previous day;

Change the time if different.

   (b) no later than 30 minutes after the requesting party was informed of the decision on that day.
   This changes rule 66.

16.8 On the last scheduled day of racing a request for redress based on a [protest committee] [jury] decision shall be delivered no later than 30 minutes after the decision was posted. This changes rule 62.2.

Include only if the protest committee is an international jury or another provision of rule 70.5 applies.

16.9 Decisions of the [protest committee] [jury] will be final as provided in rule 70.5.

17 SCORING

Include only if the Low Point System is replaced by the Bonus Point System.

17.1* The Bonus Point System of Appendix A will apply.

(OR)

Include only if neither of the Appendix A scoring systems will be used. Describe the system.

17.1* The scoring system is as follows: _____.

Insert the number.

17.2* _____ races are required to be completed to constitute a series.

Insert the numbers throughout.

17.3 (a) When fewer than _____ races have been completed, a boat's series score will be the total of her race scores.

(b) When from _____ to _____ races have been completed, a boat's series score will be the total of her race scores excluding her worst score.

(c) When _____ or more races have been completed, a boat's series score will be the total of her race scores excluding her two worst scores.

18 SAFETY REGULATIONS

Insert the procedure for check-out and check-in.

18.1 Check-Out and Check-In: _____.

18.2 A boat that retires from a race shall notify the race committee as soon as possible.

19 REPLACEMENT OF CREW OR EQUIPMENT

19.1 Substitution of competitors will not be allowed without prior written approval of the [race committee] [protest committee] [jury].

19.2 Substitution of damaged or lost equipment will not be allowed unless authorized by the [race committee] [protest committee] [jury]. Requests for substitution shall be made to the committee at the first reasonable opportunity.

20 EQUIPMENT AND MEASUREMENT CHECKS

A boat or equipment may be inspected at any time for compliance with the class rules and sailing instructions. On the water, a boat can be instructed by a race committee equipment inspector or measurer to proceed immediately to a designated area for inspection.

See ISAF Regulation 20.3(d). Insert necessary information on the advertising material.

21 ADVERTISING

Boats [shall] [may] display advertising supplied by the organizing authority as follows: _____.

Insert the descriptions. If appropriate, use different identification markings for boats performing different duties.

22 OFFICIAL BOATS

Official boats will be marked as follows: _____.

23 SUPPORT BOATS

23.1 Team leaders, coaches and other support personnel shall stay outside areas where boats are racing from the time of the preparatory signal for the first class to start until all boats have finished or retired or the race committee signals a postponement, general recall or abandonment.

Insert the identification markings. National letters are suggested for international events.

23.2 Support boats shall be marked with _____.

24 TRASH DISPOSAL

Boats shall not put trash in the water. Trash may be placed aboard support and race committee boats.

25 HAUL-OUT RESTRICTIONS

Keelboats shall not be hauled out during the regatta except with and according to the terms of prior written permission of the race committee.

26 DIVING EQUIPMENT AND PLASTIC POOLS

Underwater breathing apparatus and plastic pools or their equivalent shall not be used around keelboats between the preparatory signal of the first race and the end of the regatta.

Insert any alternative text that applies. Describe the radio communication bands or frequencies that will be used or allowed.

27 RADIO COMMUNICATION

Except in an emergency, a boat shall neither make radio transmissions while racing nor receive radio communications not available to all boats. This restriction also applies to mobile telephones.

If perpetual trophies will be awarded state their complete names.

28 PRIZES

Prizes will be given as follows: _____.

The laws applicable to the venue in which the event is held may limit disclaimers. Any disclaimer should be drafted to comply with those laws.

29 DISCLAIMER OF LIABILITY

Competitors participate in the regatta entirely at their own risk. See rule 4, Decision to Race. The organizing authority will not accept any liability for material damage or personal injury or death sustained in conjunction with or prior to, during, or after the regatta.

Insert the currency and amount.

30 INSURANCE

Each participating boat shall be insured with valid third-party liability insurance with a minimum cover of _____ per event or the equivalent.

Addendum A – Illustrating the Course

Shown here are diagrams of course shapes. The boat's track is represented by a discontinuous line so that each diagram can describe courses with different numbers of laps. If more than one course may be used for a class, state how each particular course will be signalled.

A Windward-Leeward Course

Start – 1 – 2 – 1 – 2 – Finish

Options for this course include

(1) *increasing or decreasing the number of laps,*

(2) *deleting the last windward leg,*

(3) *using a gate instead of a leeward mark,*

(4) *using an offset mark at the windward mark, and*

(5) *using the leeward and windward marks as starting and finishing marks.*

A Windward-Leeward-Triangle Course

Start – 1 – 2 – 3 – 1 – 3 – Finish

Options for this course include

(1) *increasing or decreasing the number of laps,*

(2) *deleting the last windward leg,*

(3) *varying the interior angles of the triangle (45°–90°–45° and 60°–60°–60° are common),*

(4) *using a gate instead of a leeward mark for downwind legs,*

(5) *using an offset mark at the beginning of downwind legs, and*

(6) *using the leeward and windward marks as starting and finishing marks.*

Be sure to specify the interior angle at each mark.

Trapezoid Courses

Start – 1 – 2 – 3 – 2 – 3 – Finish

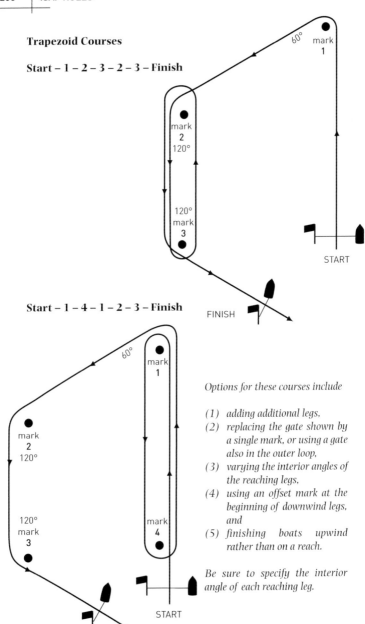

Start – 1 – 4 – 1 – 2 – 3 – Finish

Options for these courses include

(1) adding additional legs,
(2) replacing the gate shown by a single mark, or using a gate also in the outer loop,
(3) varying the interior angles of the reaching legs,
(4) using an offset mark at the beginning of downwind legs, and
(5) finishing boats upwind rather than on a reach.

Be sure to specify the interior angle of each reaching leg.

Addendum B – Boats Provided by the Organizing Authority

The following sailing instruction is recommended when all boats will be provided by the organizing authority. It can be changed to suit the circumstances. When used, it should be inserted after instruction 3.

4 BOATS

4.1 Boats will be provided for all competitors, who shall not modify them or cause them to be modified in any way except that

(a) a compass may be tied or taped to the hull or spars;

(b) wind indicators, including yarn or thread, may be tied or taped anywhere on the boat;

(c) hulls, centreboards and rudders may be cleaned, but only with water;

(d) adhesive tape may be used anywhere above the water line; and

(e) all fittings or equipment designed to be adjusted may be adjusted, provided that the class rules are complied with.

4.2 All equipment provided with the boat for sailing purposes shall be in the boat while afloat.

4.3 The penalty for not complying with one of the above instructions will be disqualification from all races sailed in which the instruction was broken.

4.4 Competitors shall report any damage or loss of equipment, however slight, to the organizing authority's representative immediately after securing the boat ashore. The penalty for breaking this instruction, unless the [protest committee] [jury] is satisfied that the competitor made a determined effort to comply, will be disqualification from the race most recently sailed.

4.5 Class rules requiring competitors to be members of the class association will not apply.

APPENDIX M – RECOMMENDATIONS FOR PROTEST COMMITTEES

This appendix is advisory only; in some circumstances changing these procedures may be advisable. It is addressed primarily to protest committee chairmen but may also help judges, protest committee secretaries, race committees and others connected with protest and redress hearings.

In a protest or redress hearing, the protest committee should weigh all testimony with equal care; should recognize that honest testimony can vary, and even be in conflict, as a result of different observations and recollections; should resolve such differences as best it can; should recognize that no boat or competitor is guilty until a breach of a *rule* has been established to the satisfaction of the protest committee; and should keep an open mind until all the evidence has been heard as to whether a boat or competitor has broken a *rule*.

M1 PRELIMINARIES (may be performed by race office staff)

● Receive the *protest* or request for redress.
● Note on the form the time the *protest* or request is delivered and the protest time limit.
● Inform each *party*, and the race committee when necessary, when and where the hearing will be held.

M2 BEFORE THE HEARING
Make sure that

● each *party* has a copy of or the opportunity to read the protest or request for redress and has had reasonable time to prepare for the hearing.
● no member of the protest committee is an *interested party*. Ask the *parties* whether they object to any member. When redress is requested under rule 62.1(a), a member of the race committee should not be a member of the protest committee.
● only one person from each boat (or *party*) is present unless an interpreter is needed.

- all boats and people involved are represented. If they are not, however, the committee may proceed under rule 63.3(b).
- boats' representatives were on board when required (rule 63.3(a)). When the *parties* were in different races, both organizing authorities must accept the composition of the protest committee (rule 63.8). In a measurement *protest* obtain the current class rules and identify the authority responsible for interpreting them (rule 64.3(b)).

M3   THE HEARING

M3.1   Check the validity of the *protest* or request for redress.

- Are the contents adequate (rule 61.2 or 62.1)?
- Was it delivered in time? If not, is there good reason to extend the time limit (rule 61.3 or 62.2)?
- When required, was the protestor involved in or a witness to the incident (rule 60.1(a))?
- When necessary, was 'Protest' hailed and, if required, a red flag displayed correctly (rule 61.1(a))?
- When the flag or hail was not necessary, was the protestee informed?
- Decide whether the *protest* or request for redress is valid (rule 63.5).
- Once the validity of the *protest* or request has been determined, do not let the subject be introduced again unless truly new evidence is available.

M3.2   Take the evidence (rule 63.6).

- Ask the protestor and then the protestee to tell their stories. Then allow them to question one another. In a redress matter, ask the *party* to state the request.
- Invite questions from protest committee members.
- Make sure you know what facts each *party* is alleging before calling any witnesses. Their stories may be different.
- Allow anyone, including a boat's crew, to give evidence. It is the *party* who normally decides which witnesses to call, although the protest committee may also call witnesses (rule 63.6). The question asked by a *party* 'Would you like to hear N?' is best answered by 'It is your choice.'
- Call each party's witnesses (and the protest committee's if

any) one by one. Limit *parties* to questioning the witness(es) (they may wander into general statements).

- Invite the protestee to question the protestor's witness first (and vice versa). This prevents the protestor from leading his witness from the beginning.
- Allow a member of the protest committee who saw the incident to give evidence (rule 63.6) but only in the presence of the *parties*. The member may be questioned and may remain in the room (rule 63.3(a)).
- Try to prevent leading questions or hearsay evidence, but if that is impossible discount the evidence so obtained.
- Accept written evidence from a witness who is not available to be questioned only if all *parties* agree. In doing so they forego their rights to question that witness (rule 63.6).
- Ask one member of the committee to note down evidence, particularly times, distances, speeds, etc.
- Invite first the protestor and then the protestee to make a final statement of her case, particularly on any application or interpretation of the *rules*.

M3.3 Find the facts (rule 63.6).

- Write down the facts; resolve doubts one way or the other.
- Call back *parties* for more questions if necessary.
- When appropriate, draw a diagram of the incident using the facts you have found.

M3.4 Decide the *protest* or request for redress (rule 64).

- Base the decision on the facts found (if you cannot, find some more facts).
- In redress cases, make sure that no further evidence is needed from boats that will be affected by the decision.

M3.5 Inform the parties (rule 65).

- Recall the *parties* and read them the facts found, conclusions and *rules* that apply, and the decision. When time presses it is permissible to read the decision and give the details later.
- Give any *party* a copy of the decision on request. File the *protest* or request for redress with the committee records.

M4 **REOPENING A HEARING (rule 66)**

When a *party*, within the time limit, has asked for a hearing to be reopened, hear the *party* making the request, look at any video, etc., and decide whether there is any material new evidence that might lead you to change your decision. Decide whether your interpretation of the *rules* may have been wrong; be open-minded as to whether you have made a mistake. If none of these applies refuse to reopen; otherwise schedule a hearing.

M5 **GROSS MISCONDUCT (rule 69)**

M5.1 An action under this rule is not a *protest*, but the protest committee gives its allegations in writing to the competitor before the hearing. The hearing is conducted under the same rules as other hearings but the protest committee must have at least three members (rule 69.1(b)). Use the greatest care to protect the competitor's rights.

M5.2 A competitor or a boat cannot protest under rule 69, but the protest form of a competitor who tries to do so may be accepted as a report to the protest committee, which can then decide whether or not to call a hearing.

M5.3 When it is desirable to call a hearing under rule 69 as a result of a Part 2 incident, it is important to hear any boat-vs.-boat *protest* in the normal way, deciding which boat, if any, broke which *rule*, before proceeding against the competitor under this rule.

M5.4 Although action under rule 69 is taken against a competitor, not a boat, a boat may also be penalized (rule 69.1(b)).

M5.5 The protest committee may warn the competitor (rule 69.1(b)(1)), in which case no report is to be made (rule 69.1(c)). When a penalty is imposed and a report is made as required by rule 69.1(c) or 69.1(e), it may be helpful to recommend whether or not further action should be taken.

M6 **APPEALS (rule 70 and Appendix F)**

When decisions can be appealed,

● retain the papers relevant to the hearing so that the information can easily be used for an appeal. Is there a

diagram endorsed or prepared by the protest committee?
Are the facts found sufficient? (Example: Was there an
overlap? Yes or No. 'Perhaps' is not a fact found.) Are the
names of the protest committee members and other
important information on the form?

● comments by the protest committee on any appeal should
enable the appeals committee to picture the whole incident clearly; the appeals committee knows nothing about
the situation.

M7   PHOTOGRAPHIC EVIDENCE

Photographs and videotapes can sometimes provide useful evidence but protest committees should recognize their
limitations and note the following points:

● The *party* producing the photographic evidence is responsible for arranging the viewing.

● View the tape several times to extract all the information
from it.

● The depth perception of any single-lens camera is very
poor; with a telephoto lens it is non-existent. When the
camera views two *overlapped* boats at right angles to their
course, it is impossible to assess the distance between them.
When the camera views them head on, it is impossible to
see whether an *overlap* exists unless it is substantial.

● Ask the following questions:
  – Where was the camera in relation to the boats?
  – Was the camera's platform moving? If so in what
    direction and how fast?
  – Is the angle changing as the boats approach the crit-
    ical point? Fast panning causes radical change.
  – Did the camera have an unrestricted view throughout?

APPENDIX N – INTERNATIONAL JURIES

*See rules 70.5 and 91(b). This appendix shall not be changed by
sailing instructions or national prescriptions.*

N1   COMPOSITION, APPOINTMENT AND ORGANIZATION

N1.1   An international jury shall be composed of experienced sailors with excellent knowledge of the racing rules and extensive protest committee experience. It shall be independent of and have no members from the race committee, and be appointed by the organizing authority, subject to approval by the national authority if required (see rule 91(b)), or by the ISAF under rule 89.2(b).

N1.2   The jury shall consist of a chairman, a vice chairman if desired, and other members for a total of at least five. A majority shall be International Judges. The jury may appoint a secretary, who shall not be a member of the jury.

N1.3   No more than two members (three, in Groups M, N and Q) shall be from the same national authority.

N1.4   (a)   The chairman of a jury may appoint one or more panels composed in compliance with rules N1.1, N1.2 and N1.3. This can be done even if the full jury is not composed in compliance with these rules.

(b)   The chairman of a jury of fewer than ten members may appoint two or three panels of at least three members each, of which the majority shall be International Judges. Members of each panel shall be from at least three different national authorities except in Groups M, N and Q, where they shall be from at least two different national authorities. If dissatisfied with a panel's decision, a *party* is entitled to a hearing by a panel composed in compliance with rules N1.1, N1.2 and N1.3, except concerning the facts found, if requested within the time limit specified in the sailing instructions.

N1.5   When a full jury, or a panel, has fewer than five members, because of illness or emergency, and no qualified replacements are available, it remains properly constituted if it consists of at least three members and if at least two of them are International Judges. When there are three or four members they shall be from at least three different national authorities except in Groups M, N and Q, where they shall be from at least two different national authorities.

N1.6   When the national authority's approval is required for the appointment of an international jury (see rule 91(b)), notice of its approval shall be included in the sailing instructions or be posted on the official notice board.

N1.7 If the jury or a panel acts while not properly constituted, its decisions may be appealed.

N2 RESPONSIBILITIES

N2.1 An international jury is responsible for hearing and deciding all *protests*, requests for redress and other matters arising under the rules of Part 5. When asked by the organizing authority or the race committee, it shall advise and assist them on any matter directly affecting the fairness of the competition.

N2.2 Unless the organizing authority directs otherwise, the jury shall decide

(a) questions of eligibility, measurement or boat certificates; and

(b) whether to authorize the substitution of competitors, boats or equipment when a *rule* requires such a decision.

N2.3 The jury shall also decide matters referred to it by the organizing authority or the race committee.

N3 PROCEDURES

N3.1 Decisions of the jury, or of a panel, shall be made by a simple majority vote of all members. When there is an equal division of votes cast, the chairman of the meeting may cast an additional vote.

N3.2 When it is considered desirable that some members not participate in discussing and deciding a *protest* or request for redress, and no qualified replacements are available, the jury or panel remains properly constituted if at least three members remain and at least two of them are International Judges.

N3.3 Members shall not be regarded as *interested parties* (see rule 63.4) by reason of their nationality.

N3.4 If a panel fails to agree on a decision it may adjourn, in which case the chairman shall refer the matter to a properly constituted panel with as many members as possible, which may be the full jury.

APPENDIX P – SPECIAL PROCEDURES FOR RULE 42

All or part of this appendix applies only if the sailing instructions so state.

P1   SIGNALLING A PENALTY

A member of the protest committee or its designated observer who sees a boat breaking rule 42 may penalize her by, as soon as reasonably possible, making a sound signal, pointing a yellow flag at her and hailing her sail number, even if she is no longer *racing*. A boat so penalized shall not be penalized a second time under rule 42 for the same incident.

P2   PENALTIES

P2.1   First Penalty

When a boat is first penalized under rule P1 her penalty shall be a Two-Turns Penalty under rule 44.2. If she fails to take it she shall be disqualified without a hearing.

P2.2   Second Penalty

When a boat is penalized a second time during the regatta, her penalty shall be to promptly retire from the race. If she fails to take it she shall be disqualified without a hearing and her score shall not be excluded.

P2.3   Third and Subsequent Penalties

When a boat is penalized a third or subsequent time during the regatta, she shall promptly retire from the race. If she does so her penalty shall be disqualification without a hearing and her score shall not be excluded. If she fails to do so her penalty shall be disqualification without a hearing from all races in the regatta, with no score excluded, and the protest committee shall consider calling a hearing under rule 69.1(a).

P3   POSTPONEMENT, GENERAL RECALL OR ABANDONMENT

If a boat has been penalized under rule P1 and the race committee signals a *postponement*, general recall or *abandonment*, the penalty is cancelled, but it is still counted to determine the number of times she has been penalized during the regatta.

P4   **REDRESS LIMITATION**

A boat shall not be given redress for an action by a member of the protest committee or its designated observer under rule P1 unless the action was improper due to a failure to take into account a race committee signal or a class rule.

P5   **FLAGS O AND R**

(a) If the class rules permit pumping, rocking and ooching when the wind speed exceeds a specified limit, the race committee may signal that those actions are permitted, as specified in the class rules, by displaying flag O before or with the warning signal. The flag shall be removed at the starting signal.

(b) If the wind speed exceeds the specified limit after the starting signal, the race committee may display flag O with repetitive sounds at a *mark* to signal to a boat that the actions are permitted, as specified in the class rules, after she has passed the *mark*.

(c) If the wind speed becomes less than the specified limit after flag O was displayed, the race committee may display flag R with repetitive sounds at a *mark* to signal to a boat that rule 42, as changed by the class rules, applies after she has passed the *mark*.

Received by race office: Number .... Date and time .... Signed ....

PROTEST FORM – also for requests for redress and reopening

Fill in and tick as appropriate

1. EVENT .... Organizing authority .... Date .... Race no ....

2. TYPE OF HEARING

Protest by boat against boat ❏   Request for redress by boat or race committee ❏

Protest by race committee against boat ❏   Consideration of redress by protest committee ❏

Protest by protest committee against boat ❏   Request by boat or race committee to reopen hearing ❏

Consideration of reopening by protest committee ❏

3. BOAT PROTESTING, OR REQUESTING REDRESS OR REOPENING

Class .... Fleet .... Sail no . ... Boat's name ....

Represented by .... Address .... Tel., e-mail .

4. BOAT(S) PROTESTED OR BEING CONSIDERED FOR REDRESS

Class .... Fleet .... Sail no . ... Boat's name ....

5. INCIDENT

Time and place of incident ....

Rules alleged to have been broken .... Witnesses ....

6. INFORMING PROTESTEE   How did you inform the protestee of your intention to protest?

By hailing   ❏ When? .... Word(s) used....................

By displaying a red flag   ❏ When? ....

By informing her in some other way ❏ ....Give details

7. DESCRIPTION OF INCIDENT (use another sheet if necessary)

DIAGRAM: one square = hull length; show position of boats, wind and current directions, marks

....

....

....

....

....

....

....

....

....

....

....

THIS SIDE FOR PROTEST COMMITTEE USE   Number .... Heard together with numbers ..
Fill in and tick as appropriate

Withdrawal requested ❏ ; Signature ....   Withdrawal permitted ❏

Class .... Fleet .... Race .... Protest time limit.......................

Protest, or request for redress or reopening, is within time limit ❏   Time limit extended ❏

Protestor, or party requesting redress or reopening, represented by ....

Other party, or boat being considered for redress, represented by ....

Names of witnesses ....

Interpreters ....

Remarks

No objection about interested party   ❏   ....

Written protest or request identifies incident   ❏   ....

'Protest' hailed at first reasonable opportunity   ❏   ....

No hail needed; protestee informed at first reasonable opportunity ❏   ....

Red flag conspicuously displayed at first reasonable opportunity   ❏   ....

Protest or request valid; hearing will continue ❏   Protest or request invalid; hearing is closed ❏

FACTS FOUND ....

....

....

....

....

....

....

Diagram of boat .... is endorsed by committee ❑   Committee's diagram is attached ❑

CONCLUSIONS AND RULES THAT APPLY

....

....

....

DECISION

Protest: dismissed ❑   Boat(s) .... is (are) disqualified from race(s) ❑ ;

                               penalized as follows ❑ : ....

Redress: not given ❑ ;   given as follows ❑ : ....

Request to reopen a hearing: denied ❑ ;   granted ❑

Protest committee chairman and other members ....

Chairman's signature .... Date and time ....

DEFINITIONS

A term used as stated below is shown in italic type or, in preambles, in bold italic type.

Abandon   A race that a race committee or protest committee *abandons* is void but may be resailed.

Clear Astern and Clear Ahead; Overlap   One boat is *clear astern* of another when her hull and equipment in normal position are behind a line abeam from the aftermost point of the other boat's hull and equipment in normal position. The other boat is *clear ahead*. They *overlap* when neither is *clear astern*. However, they also *overlap* when a boat between them *overlaps* both. These terms always apply to boats on the same *tack*. They do not apply to boats on opposite *tacks* unless rule 18 applies or both boats are sailing more than ninety degrees from the true wind.

Fetching   A boat is *fetching* a *mark* when she is in a position to pass to windward of it and leave it on the required side without changing *tack*.

Finish   A boat *finishes* when any part of her hull, or crew or equipment in normal position, crosses the finishing line in the direction of the course from the last *mark*, either for the first time or after taking a penalty under rule 44.2 or, after correcting an error made at the finishing line, under rule 28.1.

Interested Party   A person who may gain or lose as a result of a protest committee's decision, or who has a close personal interest in the decision.

Keep Clear   One boat *keeps clear* of another if the other can sail her course with no need to take avoiding action and, when the boats are *overlapped* on the same *tack*, if the *leeward* boat can change course in both directions without immediately making contact with the *windward* boat.

Leeward and Windward   A boat's *leeward* side is the side that is or, when she is head to wind, was away from the wind. However, when sailing by the lee or directly downwind, her *leeward* side is the side on which her mainsail lies. The other side is her *windward* side. When two boats on the same *tack overlap*, the one on the *leeward* side of the other is the *leeward* boat. The other is the *windward* boat.

Mark   An object the sailing instructions require a boat to leave on a specified side, and a race committee boat surrounded by navigable water from which the starting or finishing line extends. An anchor line or an object attached temporarily or accidentally to a *mark* is not part of it.

Mark-Room   *Room* for a boat to sail to the *mark*, and then *room* to sail her *proper course* while at the *mark*. However, *mark-room* does not include *room* to tack unless the boat is *overlapped* to *windward* and on the inside of the boat required to give *mark-room*.

Obstruction   An object that a boat could not pass without changing course substantially, if she were sailing directly towards it and one of her hull lengths from it. An object that can be safely passed on only one side and an area so designated by the sailing instructions are also *obstructions*. However, a boat *racing* is not an *obstruction* to other boats unless they are required to *keep clear* of her, give her *room* or *mark-room* or, if rule 22 applies, avoid her. A vessel under way, including a boat *racing*, is never a continuing *obstruction*.

Overlap   *See Clear Astern and Clear Ahead; Overlap.*

Party   A *party* to a hearing: a protestor; a protestee; a boat requesting redress; a boat or a competitor that may be penalized under rule 69.1; a race committee or an organizing authority in a hearing under rule 62.1(a).

Postpone   A *postponed* race is delayed before its scheduled start but may be started or *abandoned* later.

Proper Course   A course a boat would sail to *finish* as soon as possible in the absence of the other boats referred to in the rule using the term. A boat has no *proper course* before her starting signal.

Protest   An allegation made under rule 61.2 by a boat, a race committee or a protest committee that a boat has broken a *rule*.

Racing   A boat is *racing* from her preparatory signal until she *finishes* and clears the finishing line and *marks* or retires, or until the race committee signals a general recall, *postponement* or *abandonment*.

Room   The space a boat needs in the existing conditions while manoeuvring promptly in a seamanlike way.

Rule (a) The rules in this book, including the Definitions, Race Signals, Introduction, preambles and the rules of relevant appendices, but not titles;

(b) ISAF Regulation 19, Eligibility Code; Regulation 20, Advertising Code; Regulation 21, Anti-Doping Code; and Regulation 22, Sailor Classification Code;

(c) the prescriptions of the national authority, unless they are changed by the sailing instructions in compliance with the national authority's prescription, if any, to rule 88;

(d) the class rules (for a boat racing under a handicap or rating system, the rules of that system are 'class rules');

(e) the notice of race;

(f) the sailing instructions; and

(g) any other documents that govern the event.

Start   A boat *starts* when, having been entirely on the pre-start side of the starting line at or after her starting signal, and having complied with rule 30.1 if it applies, any part of her hull, crew or equipment crosses the starting line in the direction of the first *mark*.

Tack, Starboard or Port   A boat is on the *tack, starboard* or *port*, corresponding to her *windward* side.

Zone   The area around a *mark* within a distance of three hull lengths of the boat nearer to it. A boat is in the *zone* when any part of her hull is in the *zone*.

Windward   See **Leeward and Windward**.

RACE SIGNALS

The meanings of visual and sound signals are stated below. When a visual signal is displayed over a class flag, the signal applies only to that class.

AP   Races not started are *postponed.* The warning signal will be made 1 minute after removal unless at that time the race is postponed again or abandoned.

AP over a numeral pennant 1–6:   *Postponement* of 1–6 hours from the scheduled starting time.

AP over H: Races not started are *postponed.* Further signals ashore.

AP over A: Races not started are *postponed.* No more racing today.

C   The position of the next *mark* has been changed.

I   Rule 30.1 is in effect.

L   Ashore: A notice to competitors has been posted.
   Afloat: Come within hail or follow this boat.

M   The object displaying this signal replaces a missing *mark.*

N   All races that have started are *abandoned.* Return to the starting area. The warning signal will be made 1 minute after removal unless at that time the race is abandoned again or postponed.

N over H: All races are *abandoned.* Further signals ashore.

N over A: All races are *abandoned.* No more racing today.

P   Preparatory signal.

S   The course has been shortened. Rule 32.2 is in effect.
   At a rounding or finishing *mark: Finish* between the nearby *mark* and the staff displaying this flag.

X   Individual recall.

Y   Wear personal buoyancy.

Z   Rule 30.2 is in effect.

First substitute: General recall. The warning signal will be made 1 minute after removal.

Black flag: Rule 30.3 is in effect.

Blue flag or shape: This Race Committee boat is in position at the finishing line.